بیایید کلمه های فارسی بیاموزیم

(تمرین های کمک درسی)

Let's Learn Persian Words

A Farsi Activity Book

(A Combined Edition of Book One and Book Two)

Nazanin Mirsadeghi

Bahar Books

www.baharbooks.com

Mirsadeghi, Nazanin
    Let's Learn Persian Words: A Farsi Activity Book/ Nazanin Mirsadeghi
    (A Combined Edition of Book One & Book Two)

This book is a combined volume of Let's Learn Persian Words (Book One) & (Book Two)
Let's Learn Persian Words (Book One) Copyright © 2012 ISBN-13: 978-1939099006
Let's Learn Persian Words (Book Two) Copyright © 2012 ISBN-13: 978-1939099051

Let's Learn Persian Words (Combined Edition of Book One & Two):
ISBN-13: 978-1-939099-79-2

Copyright © 2020 by Bahar Books, LLC

Published by Bahar Books, White Plains, New York

www.baharbooks.com

بیایید کلمه های فارسی بیاموزیم

(تمرین های کمک درسی)

سخنی با خوانندگان فارسی زبان،

یکی از مشکلات آموزش زبان فارسی به کودکانی که فارسی را به عنوان زبان دوّم می آموزند دسترسی نداشتن به آن دسته از کتاب های کمک درسی ست که برای این گروه از دانش آموزان طرح ریزی شده باشند.

هدف اصلی این کتاب، فراهم آوردن تمرین هایی ست که با روش تدریس کتاب "آموزش زبان فارسی اوّل دبستان" – که منبع اصلی تدریس در اکثر مدارس فارسی در خارج از کشورست – هماهنگی داشته و در ضمن با کمک گیری از بازی ها و جدول ها، یادگیری خواندن و نوشتن کلمات تازه را برای دانش آموزان ساده تر کنند.

ترتیب حروف استفاده شده در این کتاب، هماهنگ با ترتیب تدریس این حروف در کتاب "آموزش زبان فارسی اوّل دبستان" است. به همین دلیل، این کتاب می تواند به عنوان تمرینات اضافه در کنار کتاب اصلی آموزش زبان فارسی توسط آموزگاران و پدران و مادران دانش آموزان مورد استفاده قرار گیرد.

لازم به تذکر است که تمرین های این کتاب، پیش از این در دو جلد و تحت عنوان "بیایید کلمه های فارسی بیاموزیم (کتاب اول)" و "بیایید کلمه های فارسی بیاموزیم (کتاب دوم)" منتشر شده اند.

در اینجا لازم است از خانم لادن مشتاقی که با نظرات و پیشنهادات شان من را در کار تنظیم این کتاب یاری دادند صمیمانه سپاسگزاری کنم.

نازنین میرصادقی

To English–speaking readers …

This activity book has been designed for students of Iranian Heritage that are learning Persian as a second language in a classroom. This activity book could be used as a supplement to the *Elementary Persian Language* textbook which is the main resource used in most Persian schools outside Iran. The letters used in the activities of this book are sequenced in the same order as the letters taught in the *Elementary Persian Language* textbook.

If you are learning Persian on your own, you should be familiar with the Persian alphabet and be able to read the Persian script prior to using this workbook. This practical activity book could provide you with fun and effective ways to expand your reading and writing vocabulary through a variety of activities such as puzzles, word searches and matching exercises.

It must be noted that the exercises in this book have been published previously in two separate volumes.

Many Thanks are due to Mrs. Ladan Moshtaghi for her help and support in preparing these books.

Nazanin Mirsadeghi

Pronunciation Guide for the Persian Letters

aa like the "a" in arm	‫ا – آ‬ *
b like the "b" in boy	‫بـ – ب‬
p like the "p" in play	‫پـ – پ‬
t like the "t" in tree	‫ تـ – ت‬
s like the "s" in sun	‫ ثـ – ث‬
j like the "j" in jam	‫ جـ – ج‬
ch like the "ch" in child	‫ چـ – چ‬
h like the "h" in hotel	‫ حـ – ح‬
ǩ like "ch" in the German word *bach*, or Hebrew word *smach*.	‫ خـ – خ‬
d like the "d" in door	‫د‬
z like the "z" in zebra	‫ذ‬
r like the "r" in rabbit	‫ر‬
z like the "z" in zebra	‫ز‬
ž like the "z" in zwago	‫ژ‬
s like the "s" in sun	‫ سـ – س‬
sh like the "sh" in shell	‫ شـ – ش‬
s like the "s" in sun	‫ صـ – ص‬
z like the "z" in zebra	‫ ضـ – ض‬

t like the "t" in tree	ط
z like the "z" in zebra	ظ
' is a glottal stop, like between the syllables of "uh–oh"	ع – ﻊ – ﺀ
ğ like the "r " in French word *merci*	غ – ﻎ – ﻍ
f like the "f " in fall	ف – ﻒ
ğ like the "r" in French word *merci*	ﻖ – ق
k like the "k" in kite	ک – ﻚ
g like the "g" in game	گ – ﮓ
l like the "l" in lost	ا – ل
m like the "m" in master	ﻢ – م
n like the "n" in night	ﻦ – ﻧ
v like the "v" in van	و
o like the "o" in ocean	و
On some occasions, it has no sound and becomes silent.	و
oo like the "oo" in good	او – و *
h like the "h" in hotel	ه – ﻪ – ﻬ – ﺩ
e like the "e" in element	ه – ﻪ
y like the "y" in yellow	ﻲ – ی
ee like the "ee" in need	ﺍﯾ – ﻲ – ی – ﺍی*

* long vowels

It represents doubled consonants.	ّ

a like the "a" in animal	ـَ **
o like the "o" in ocean	ـُ **
e like the "e" in element	ـِ **

** short vowels

Persian Letters with the Same Pronunciation

t like the **"t"** in tree	ت – ت
	ط
ğ like the **"r"** in French word *merci*	ق – ق
	غ – غ – غ
h like the **"h"** in hotel	ح – ح
	ه – ه – ه – ه
s like the **"s"** in sun	ث – ث
	س – س
	ص – ص
z like the **"z"** in zebra	ذ
	ز
	ض
	ظ

Names Given to the Persian Letters

alef	ا – آ
be	بِ – ب
pe	پِ – پ
te	تِ – ت
se	ثِ – ث
jeem	جِ – ج
che	چِ – چ
he	حِ – ح
ǩe	خِ – خ
daal	د
zaal	ذ
re	ر
ze	ز
že	ژ
seen	سِ – س
sheen	شِ – ش
saad	صِ – ص
zaad	ضِ – ض

taa	ط
zaa	ظ
eyn	ع – ـع – ـعـ
ğeyn	غ – ـغ – ـغـ
fe	ف – ـف
ğaaf	ق – ـق
kaaf	ک – ـک
gaaf	گ – ـگ
laam	ل – ـل
meem	م – ـم
noon	ن – ـن
vaav	و
he	ه – ـه – ـهـ – ه
ye	ی – ـی

Exercise 1

Clouds

اَبر

(abr)

Wind

باد

(baad)

Basket

سَبَد

(sa. bad)

Read the word for each picture and
write the letters in their places.

با کمک شکل ها، هر کلمه را بخوان و
صداهایش را در جدولِ روبرویش بنویس.

Wind

باد

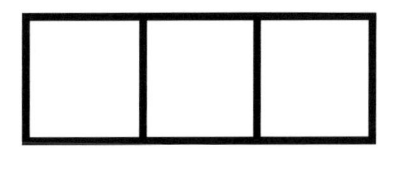

Clouds

اَبر

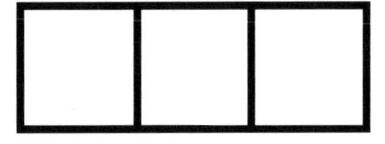

Basket

سَبَد

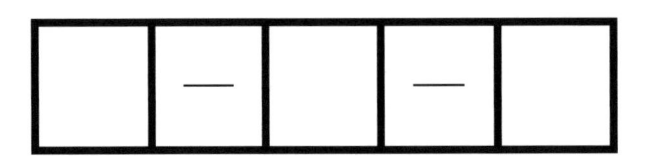

۲

Wind

اَبر

Clouds

سَبَد

Basket

باد

Read the word for each picture

با کمکِ شکل ها، هر کلمه را بخوان و جایش را

۳

and write the letters in the puzzle. در جدول پیدا کن.

Basket

سَبَد

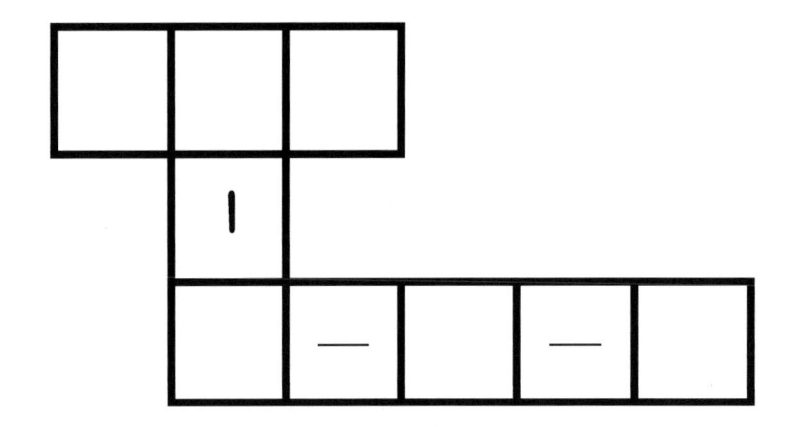

ا

Clouds

اَبر

Wind

باد

سَبَد

ن	ص	پ	سَ	ل	ا	م
ج	بِ	ا	بَ	ا	د	چ
ا	ی	ت	د	ث	بُ	ا
ل	ه	بَ	ط	شَ	ا	ن
ا	و	ن	ع	ا	ف	ص

Look at this picture and write its name
under it.

به این شکل نگاه کن و اسمش را زیر آن
بنویس.

Wind

_____

Write the letters for each word.

اَبر= __ + __ + __

باد= __ + __ + __

سَبَد= __ + __ + __ + __ + __

Read the word below and draw a picture of it.

آبر

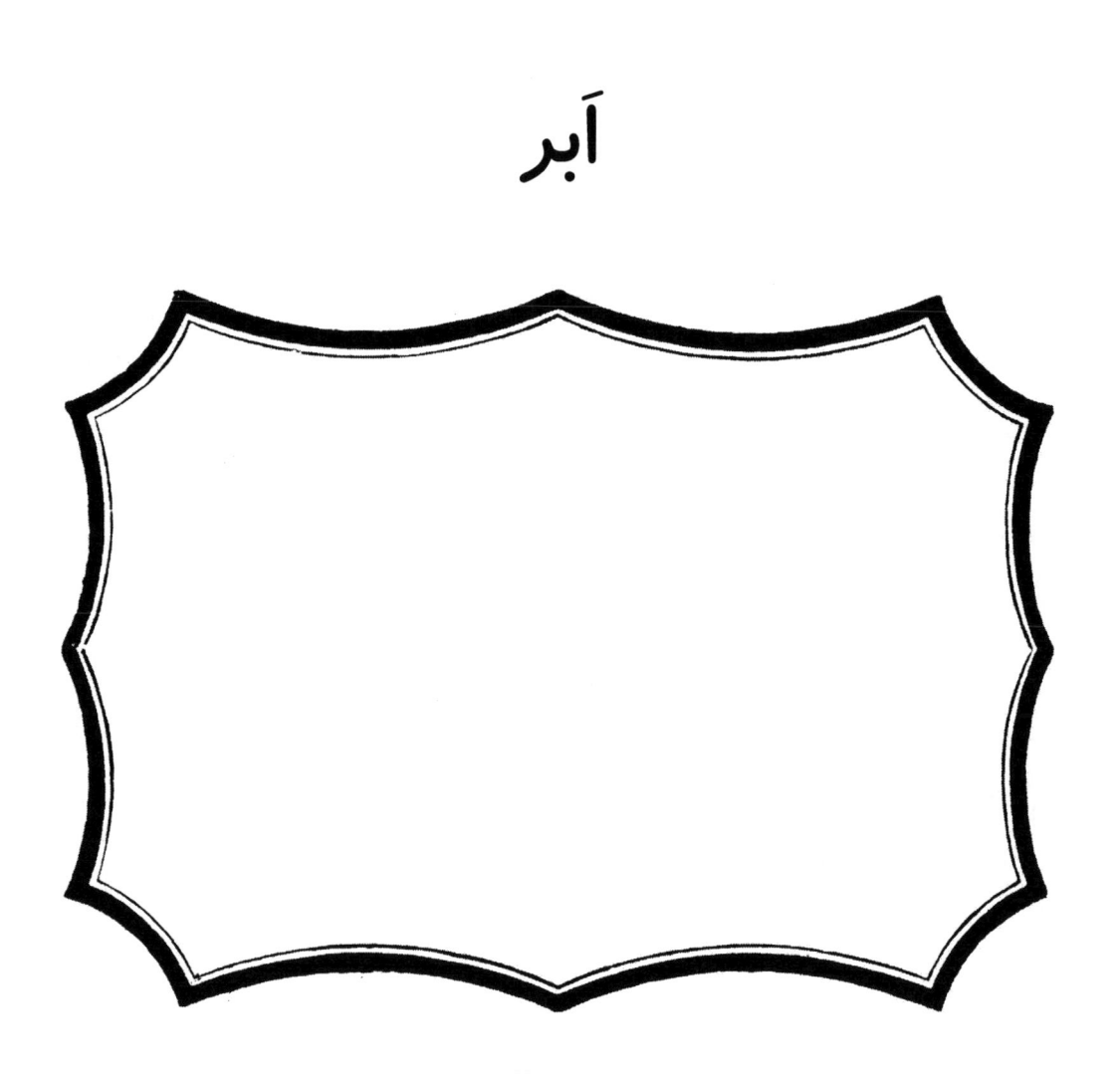

Exercise 2 تمرين ۲

Horse

اَسب

(asb)

Net

تور

(toor)

Swing

تاب

(taab)

Read the word for each picture and
write the letters in their places.

Horse

اَسب

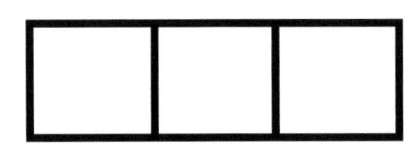

Net

تور

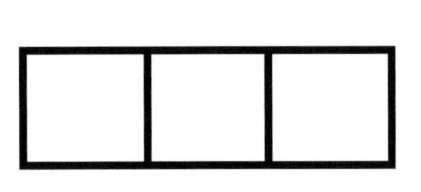

Swing

تاب

با کمک شکل ها، هر کلمه را بخوان و
صداهایش را در جدولِ روبرویش بنویس.

Horse

اَسب

Net

تور

Swing

تاب

Connect each word to its picture.

هر کلمه را به شکلش وصل کن.

تور

اَسب

اَبر

سَبَد

تاب

١١

Read the word for each picture and write the letters in the puzzle.

با کمکِ شکل ها، هر کلمه را بخوان و جایش را در جدول پیدا کن.

تور

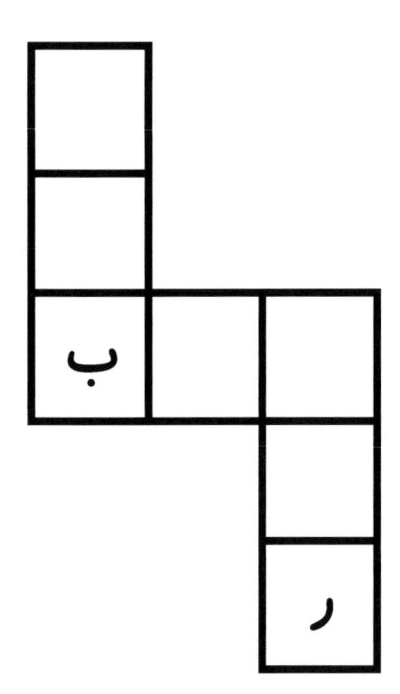

اَسب

تاب

۱۲

Find the word below in the puzzle.

اَسب

سَ	ی	ر	ت	ض	ه
ا	ب	س	اَ	ط	و
بَ	ل	اِ	ی	د	سُ
ک	ا	ش	ف	چ	و
بَ	م	اِ	ژ	ر	سُ

Look at this picture and write its name under it.

Net

_____

Write the letters for each word. صداهای هر کلمه را بنویس.

اَسب = __ + __ + __

تور = __ + __ + __

تاب = __ + __ + __

Read the word below and draw a picture of it.

كلمه زير را بخوان و شكلش را بكش.

تاب

Exercise 3

باران

(baa. raan)

اَنار

(a. naar)

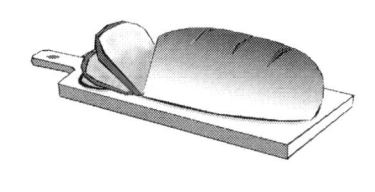

نان

(naan)

Read the word for each picture and write the letters in their places.

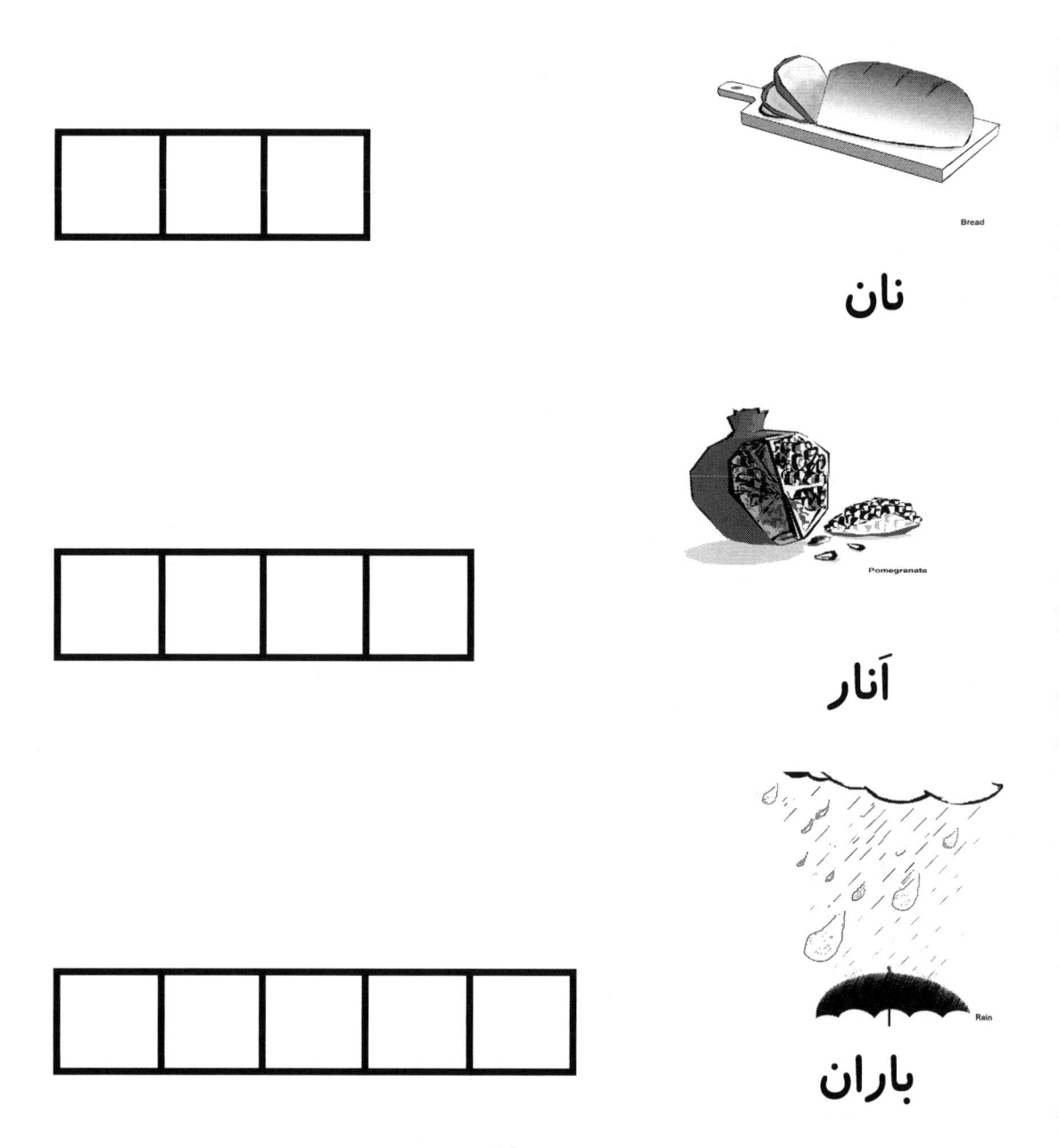

نان

آنار

باران

Connect each word to its picture.

آنار

نان

تاب

باران

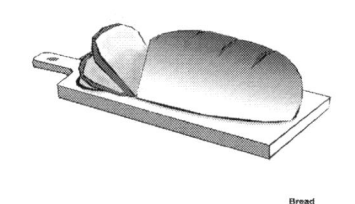

اَسب

Read the word for each picture and
write the letters in the puzzle.

باران

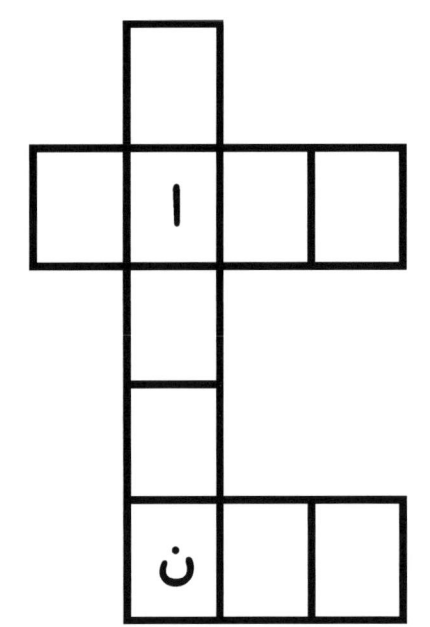

آنار

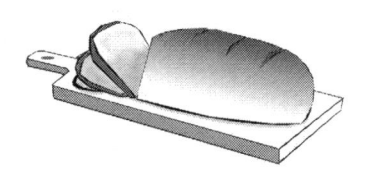

نان

۲۰

Find the word below in the puzzle.

نان

ت	ا	ن	ف	و	ت
ق	ی	ر	ذ	ش	ا
ک	ن	ی	ا	گ	ز
ل	خ	ه	ن	و	ب
ت	م	ن	ز	د	ت

Look at this picture and write its name under it.

به این شکل نگاه کن و اسمش را زیر آن بنویس.

Pomegranate

_____

Write the letters for each word.   صداهای هر کلمه را بنویس.

نان= __ + __ + __

اَنار= __ + __ + __ + __

باران= __ + __ + __ + __ + __

Read the word below and draw a picture of it.

کلمه زیر را بخوان و شکلش را بکش.

باران

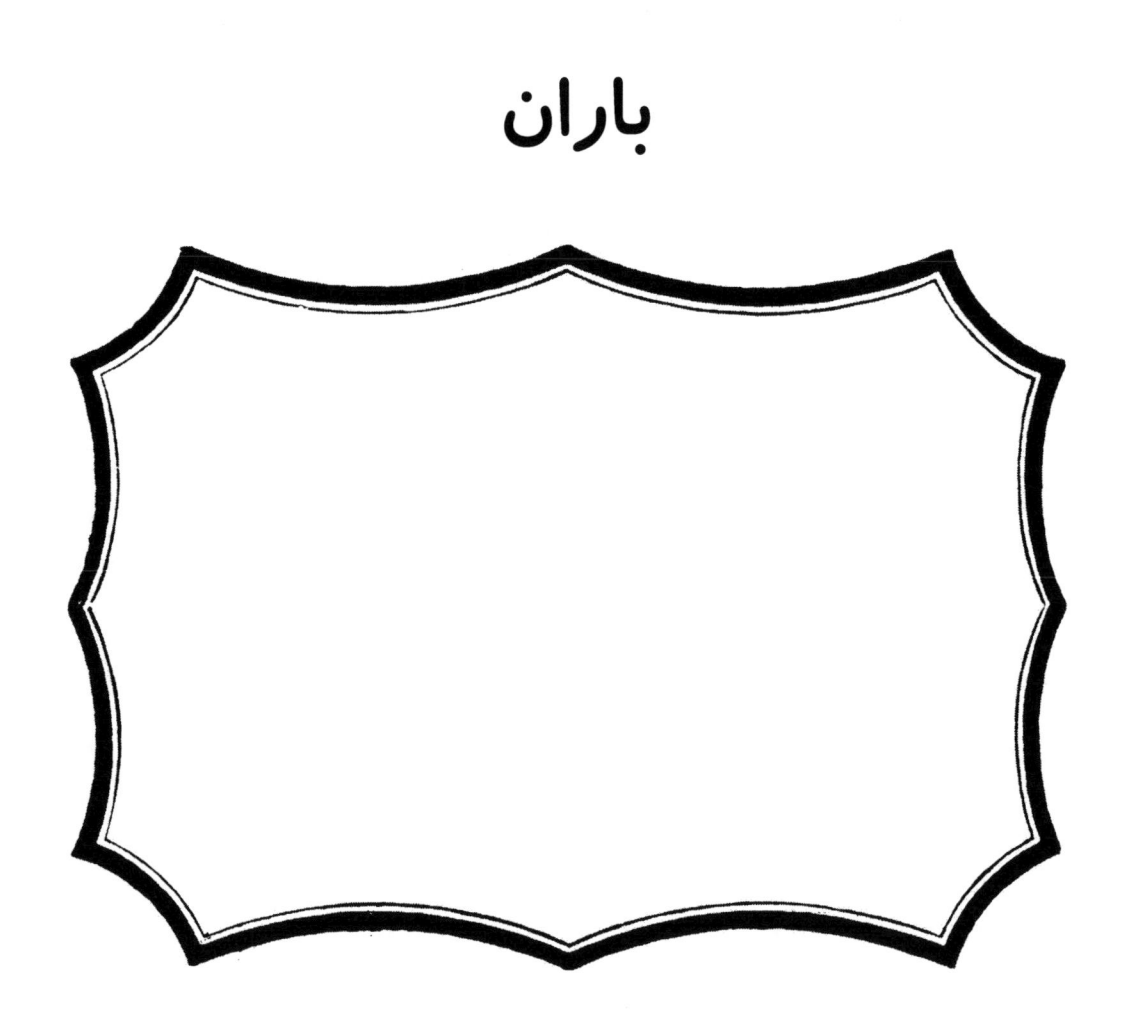

Exercise 4   تمرین ۴

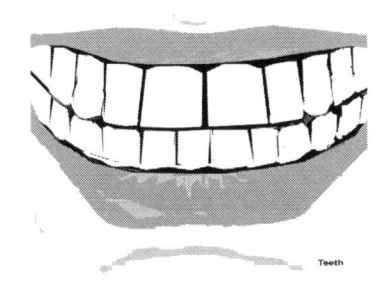

دَندان

(dan. daan)

زَبان

(za. baan)

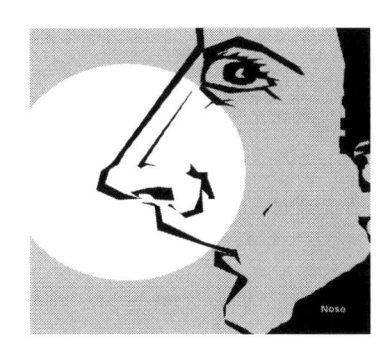

بینی

(bee. nee)

Read the word for each picture and
write the letters in their places.

با کمک شکل ها، هر کلمه را بخوان و
صداهایش را در جدولِ روبرویش بنویس.

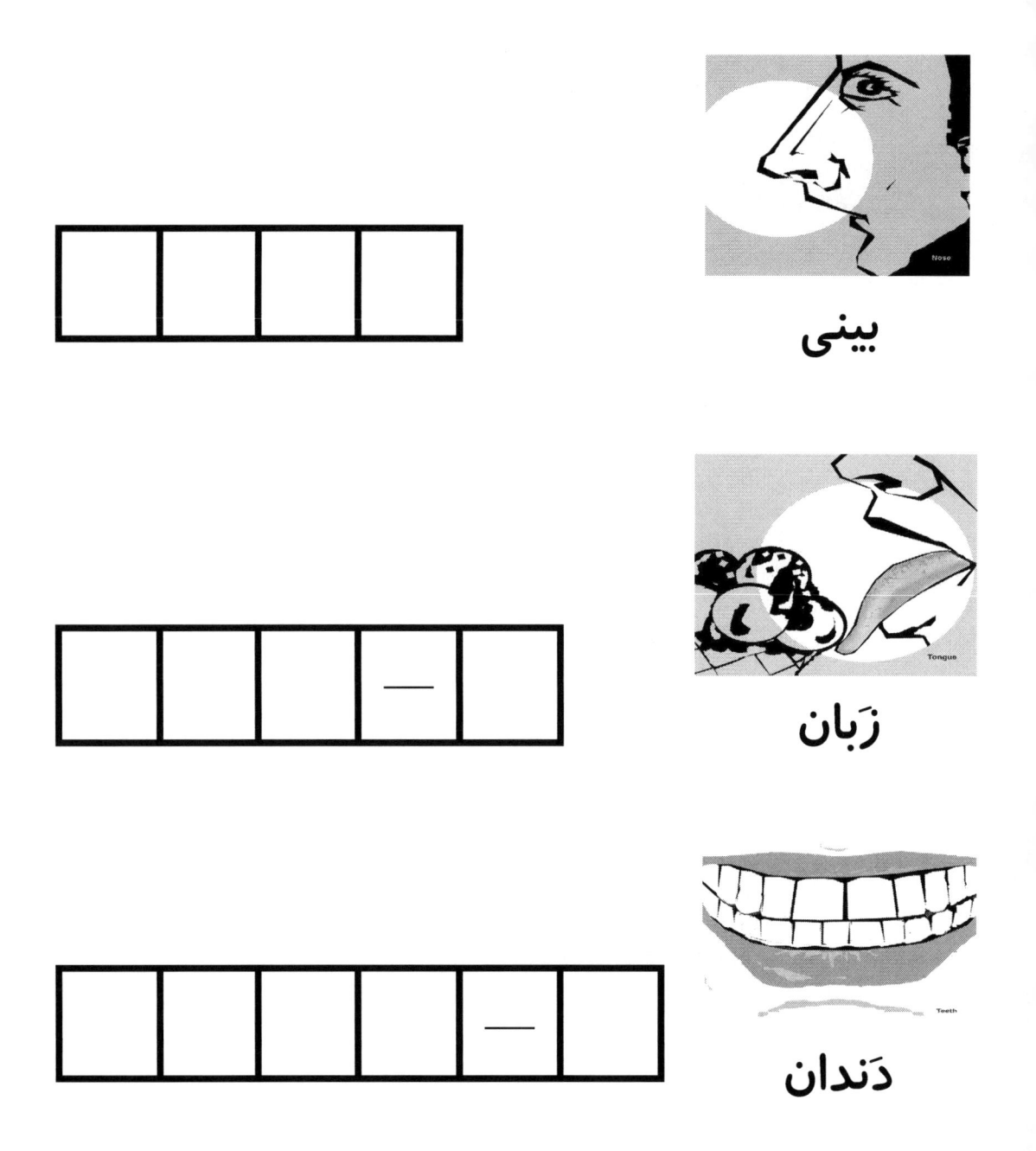

بینی

زَبان

دَندان

Connect each word to its picture.

هر کلمه را به شکلش وصل کن.

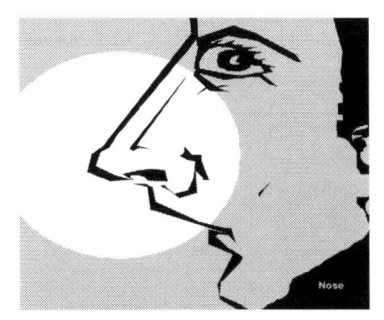

زَبان

نان

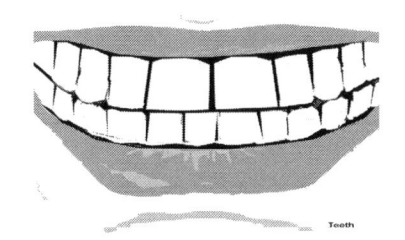

دَندان

باران

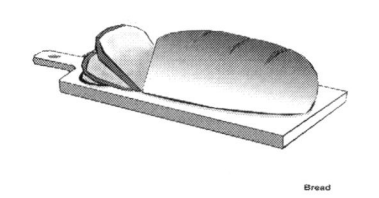

بینی

۲۷

Read the word for each picture and write the letters in the puzzle.

با کمک شکل ها، هر کلمه را بخوان و جایش را در جدول پیدا کن.

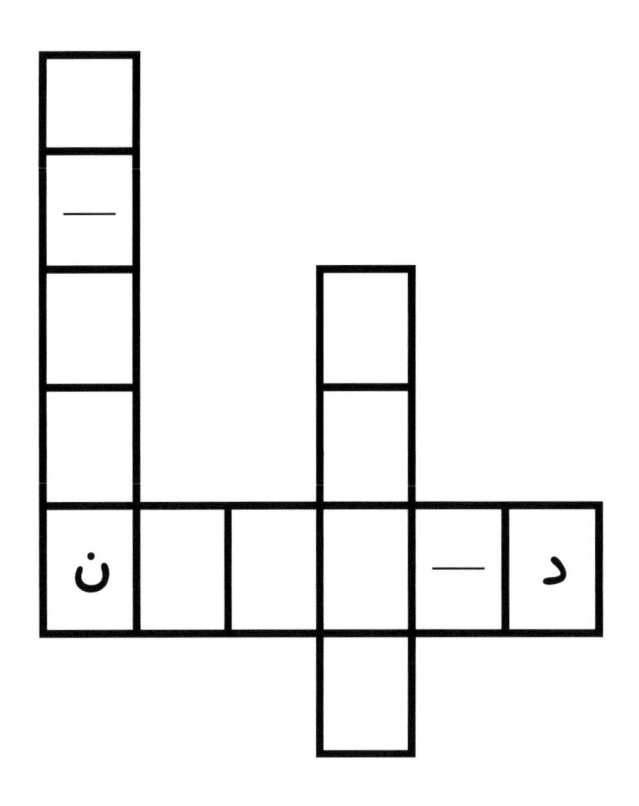

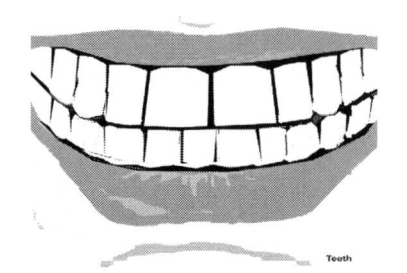

دَندان

زَبان

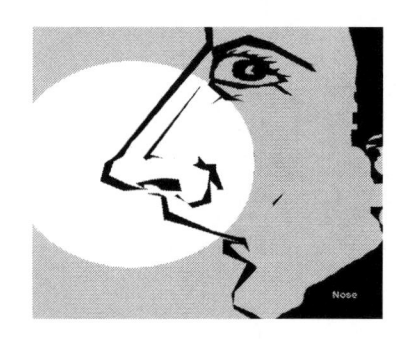

بینی

Find the word below in the puzzle. کلمه زیر را در جدول پیدا کن.

بینی

س	ز	ن	ف	پ	ز
ب	ی	ذ	یـ	بـ	ا
ش	دَ	و	ا	ز	م
ز	ذ	دَ	ل	خ	ا
ا	دَ	ذ	ی	ز	م

Look at this picture and write its name under it.

به این شکل نگاه کن و اسمش را زیر شکل بنویس.

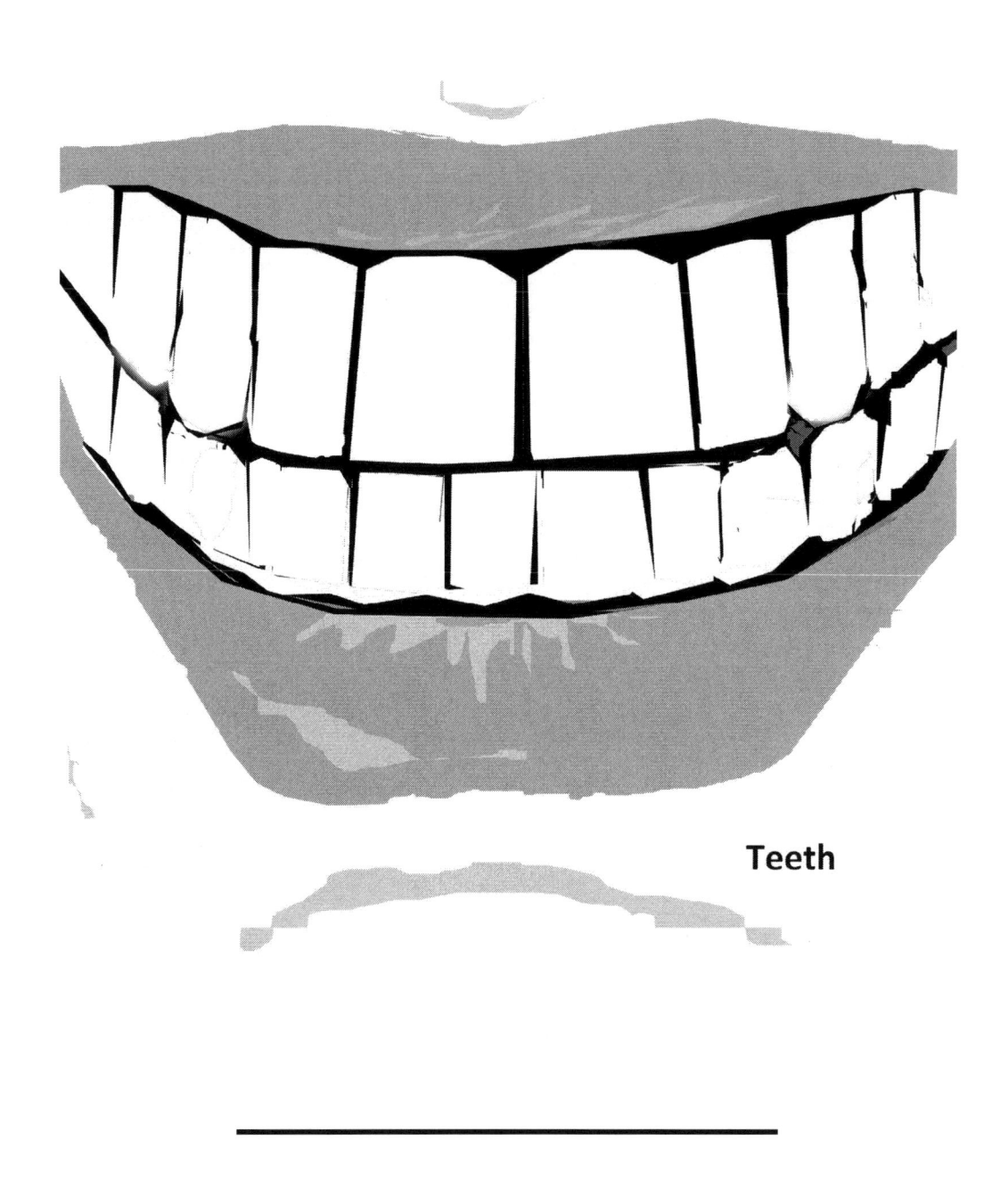

Teeth

_____

Write the letters for each word.   صداهای هر کلمه را بنویس.

__ + __ + __ + __ = بینی

__ + __ + __ + __ + __ = زَبان

__ + __ + __ + __ + __ + __ = دَندان

Read the word below and draw a picture of it.

کلمه زیر را بخوان و شکلش را بکش.

زَبان

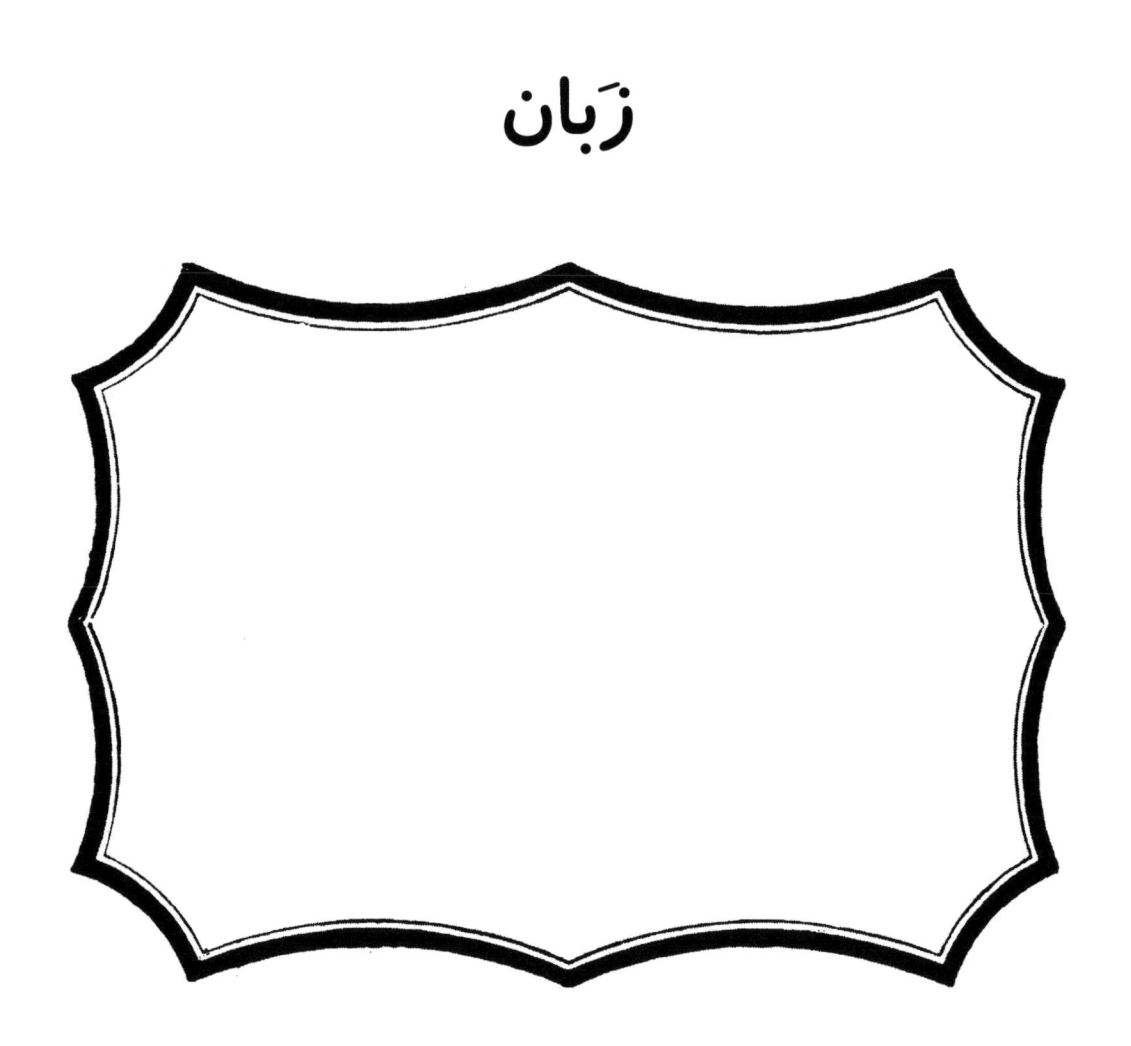

Exercise 5

تمرین ۵

شیر

(sheer)

سینی

(see. nee)

بَستَنی

(bas. ta. nee)

Read the word for each picture and
write the letters in their places.

شیر

سینی

بَستَنی

Connect each word to its picture. هر کلمه را به شکلش وصل کن.

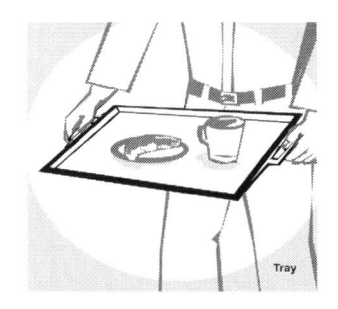

زَبان

شیر

دَندان

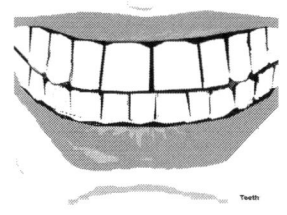

بَستَنی

سینی

Read the word for each picture and write the letters in the puzzle.

با کمک شکل ها، هر کلمه را بخوان و جایش را در جدول پیدا کن.

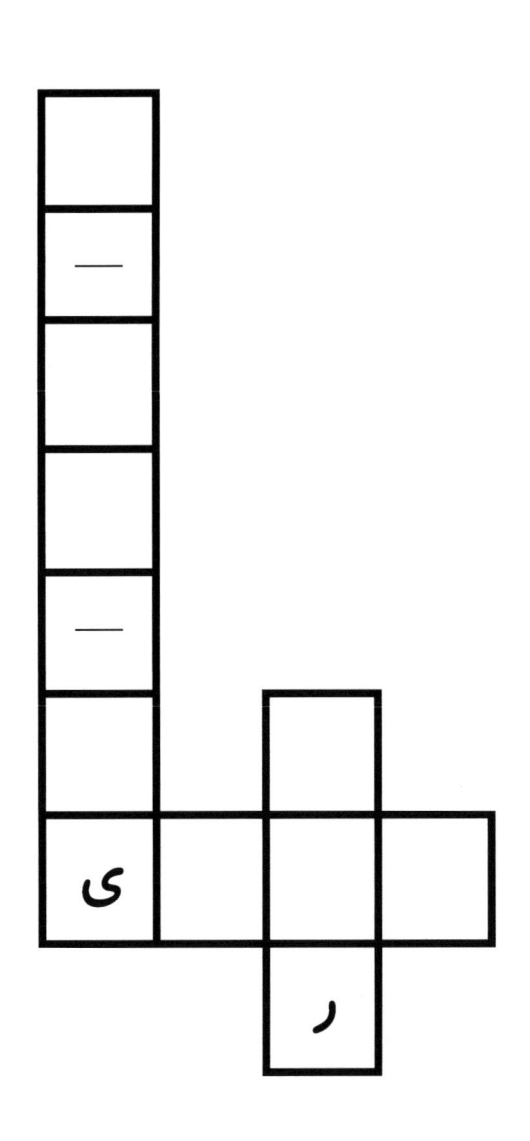

بَستَنی

شیر

سینی

Find the word below in the puzzle.

سینی

ط	ی	غ	ه	ا	ش	ت
ذ	س	زُ	دَ	ز	و	ا
ف	ي	و	ب	ا	ل	ش
پِ	ن	ی	ذِ	ی	س	و
گ	س	و	ا	ل	م	ا

Look at this picture and write its name
under it.

Milk

Write the letters for each word.

شیر = ___ + ___ + ___

سینی = ___ + ___ + ___ + ___

بَستَنی = ___ + ___ + ___ + ___ + ___ + ___ + ___

Read the word below and draw a picture of it.

بَستَنی

Exercise 6 تمرین ۶

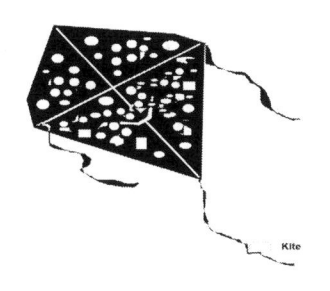

بادبادَک

(baad. baa. dak)

اُردَک

(or. dak)

کَبوتَر

(ka. boo. tar)

Read the word for each picture and write the letters in their places.

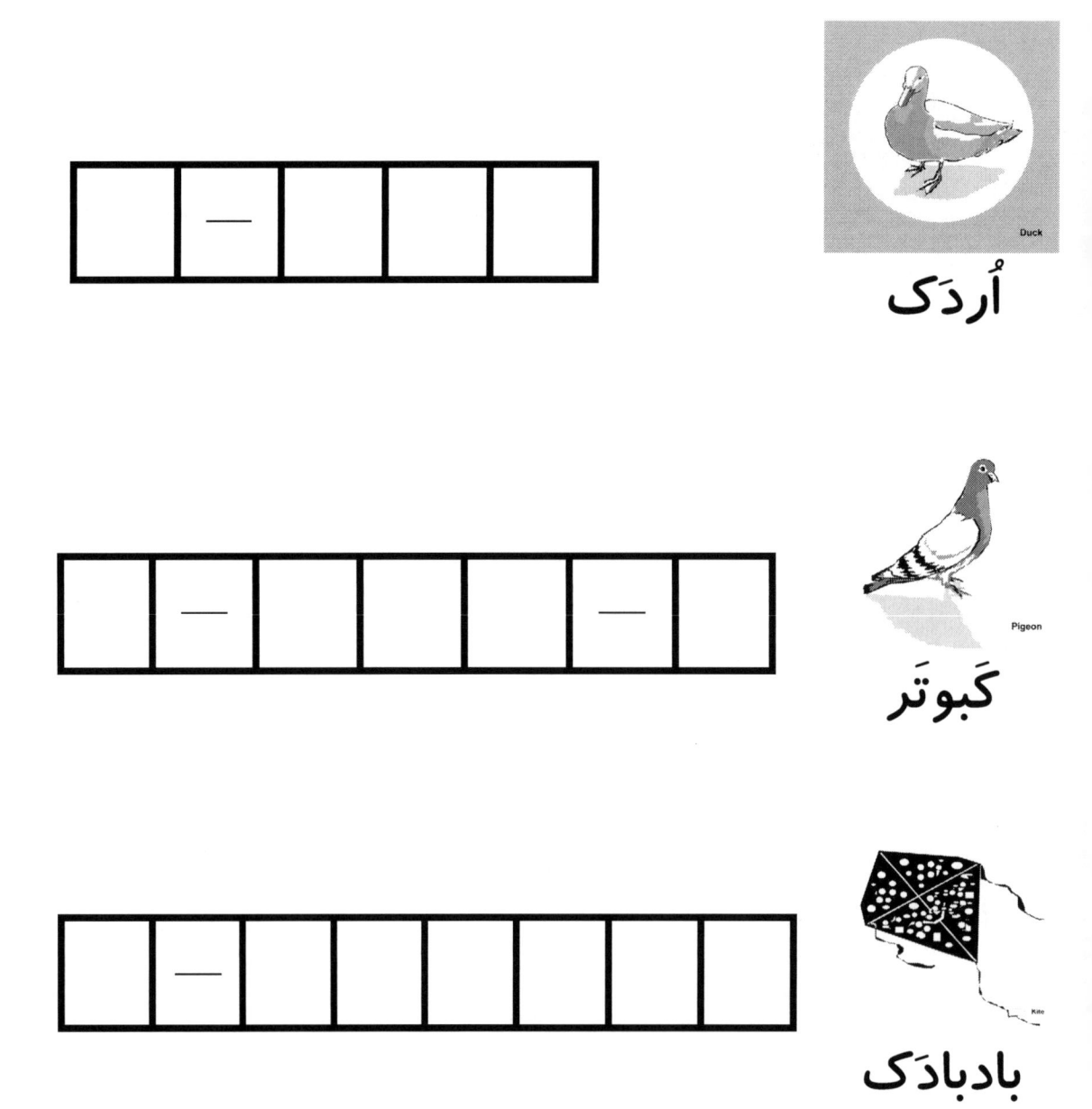

با کمک شکل ها، هر کلمه را بخوان و صداهایش را در جدولِ روبرویش بنویس.

Duck

اُردَک

Pigeon

کَبوتَر

Kite

بادبادَک

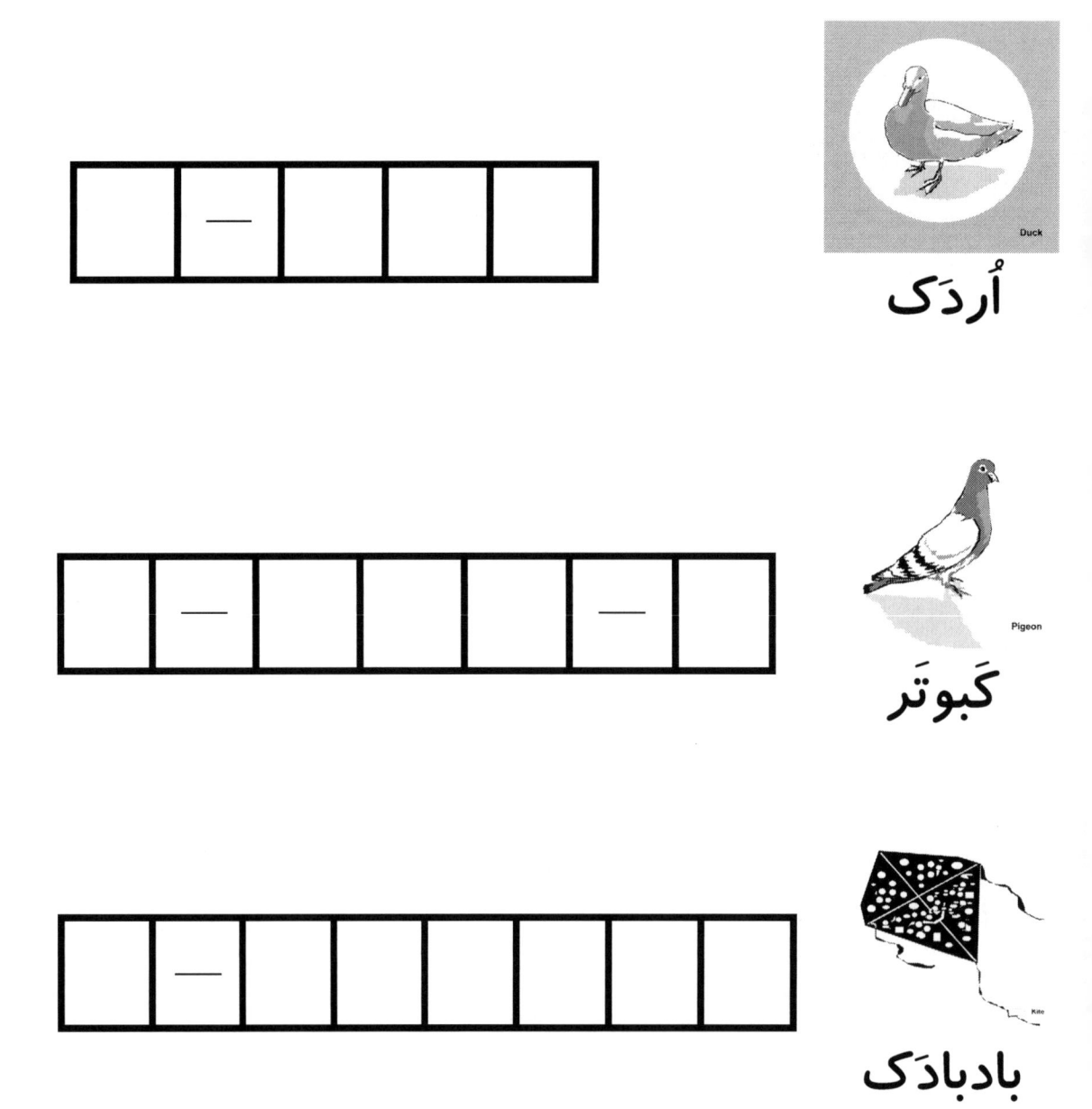

۴۲

Connect each word to its picture.

هر کلمه را به شکلش وصل کن.

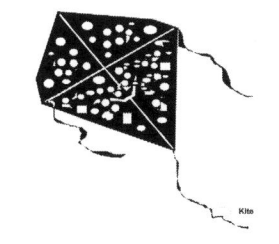

کَبوتَر

بَستَنی

شیر

اَردَک

بادبادَک

Connect each word to its picture.

هر کلمه را به شکلش وصل کن.

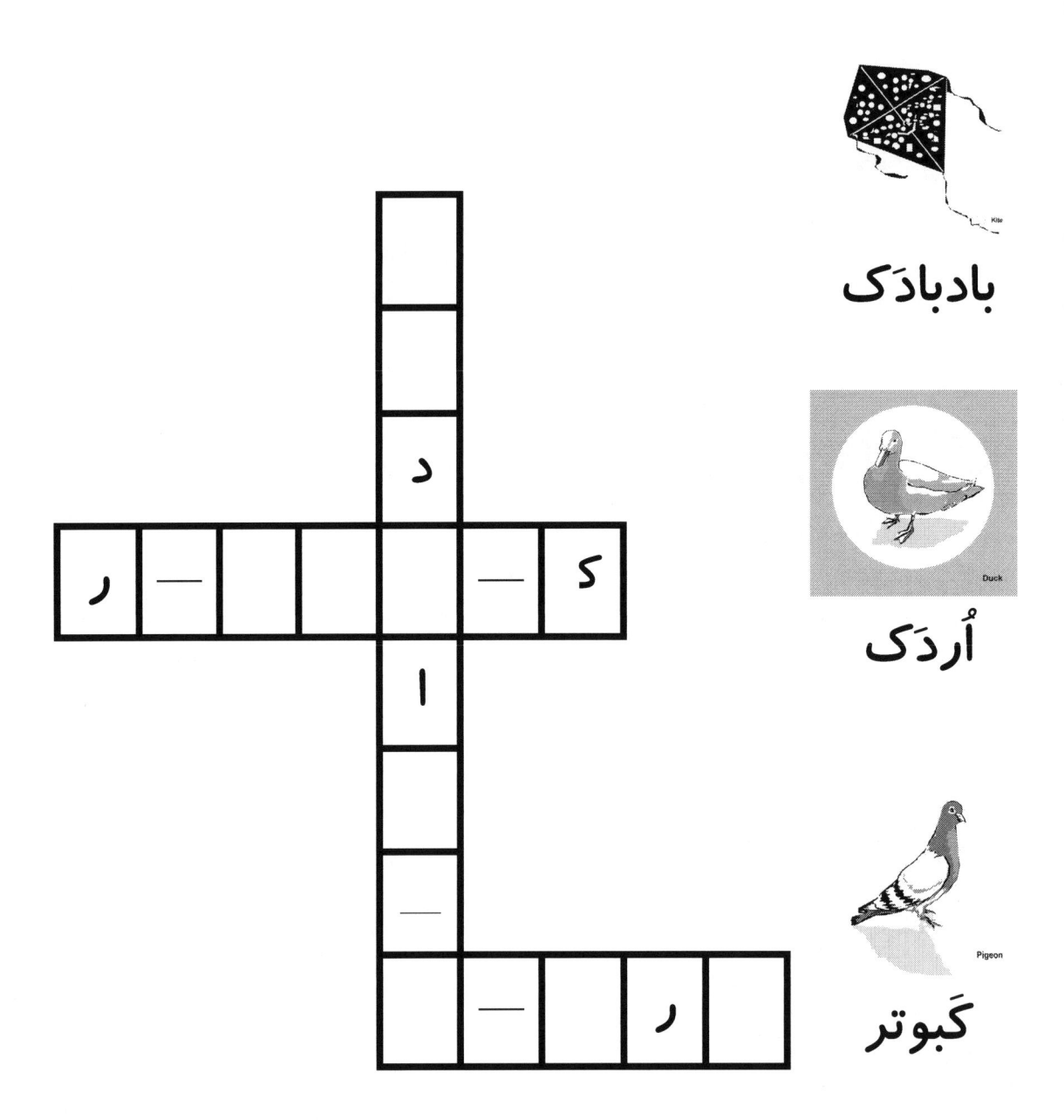

بادبادَک

اُردَک

کَبوتر

Find the word below in the puzzle.

کَبوتَر

ل	و	ز	کَ	د	م	ن
کِ	ا	ل	بِ	و	ن	ش
ا	گِ	بِ	و	ا	ز	تَ
خ	ه	و	تَ	ر	ت	بِ
کُ	ا	د	ر	ل	ا	ک

Look at this picture and write its name
under it.

به این شکل نگاه کن و اسمش را زیر آن
بنویس.

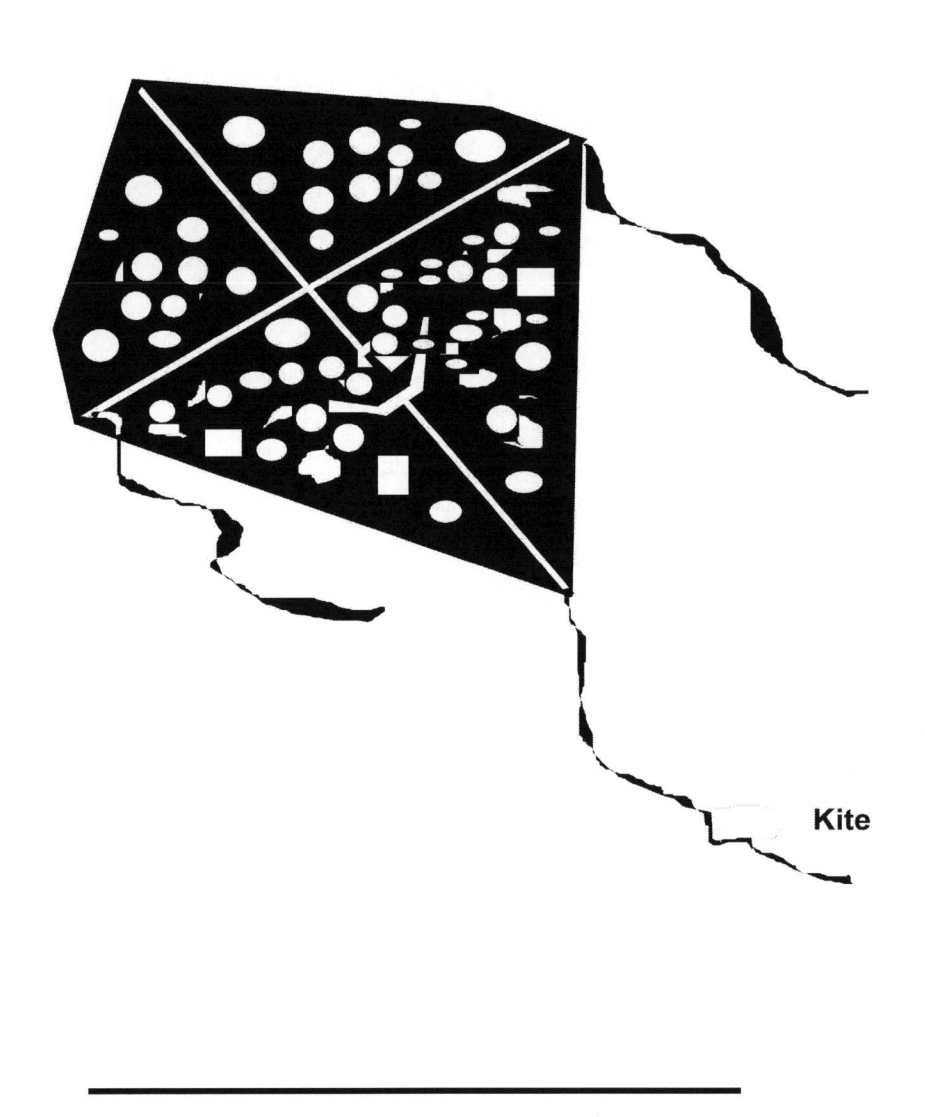

Kite

_____

صداهای هر کلمه را بنویس.

اُرَدَک= __ + __ + __ + __ + __

کَبوتَر = __ + __ + __ + __ + __ + __ + __

بادبادَک= __ + __ + __ + __ + __ + __ + __ + __

Read the word below and draw a picture of it.

اُردَک

Exercise 7   ٧ تمرین

Train

ترَن

(te. ran)

Ship

کَشتی

(kash. tee)

Car

ماشین

(maa. sheen)

Read the word for each picture and
write the letters in their places.

با کمک شکل ها، هر کلمه را بخوان و
صداهایش را در جدولِ روبرویش بنویس.

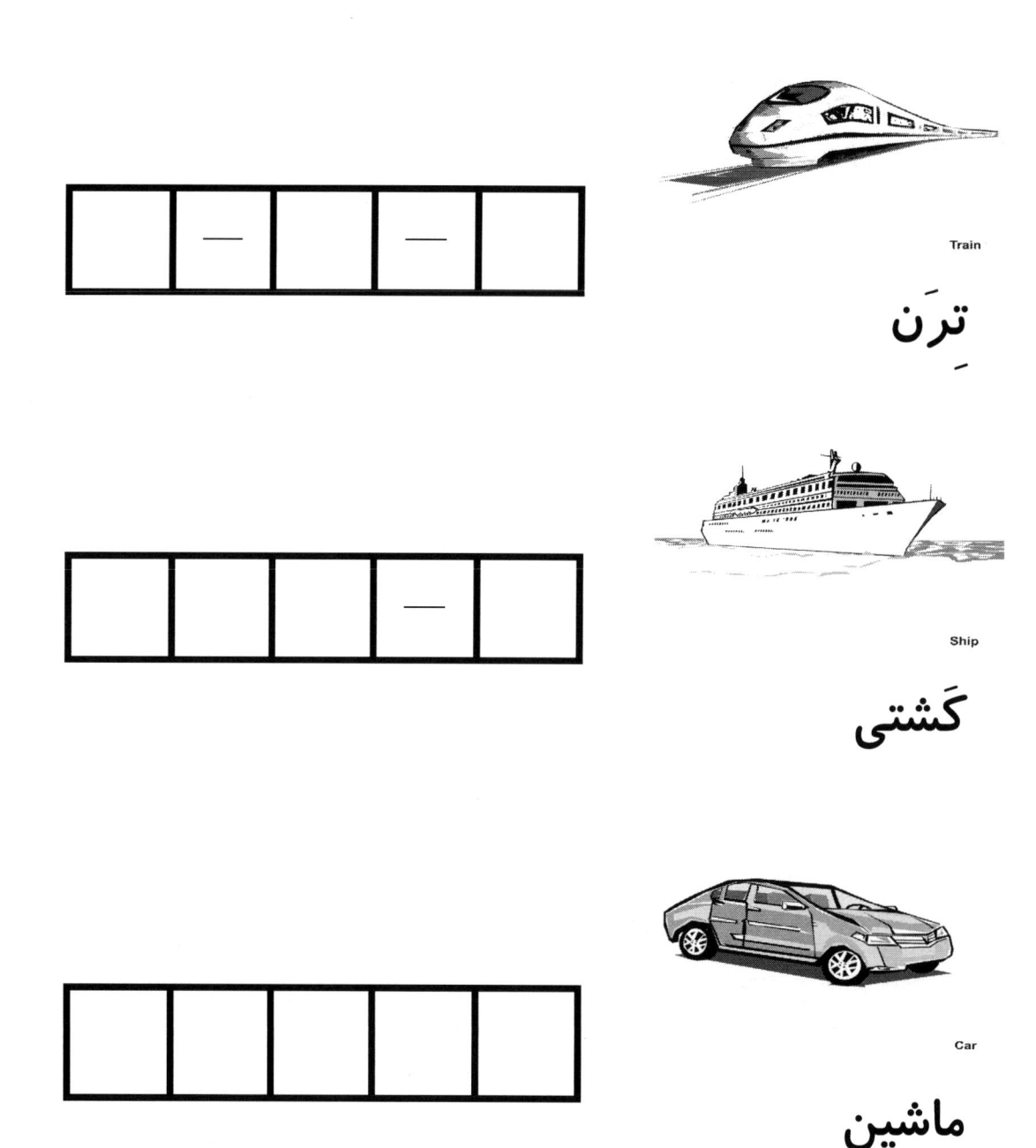

Train

ترَن

Ship

کَشتی

Car

ماشین

۵۰

Connect each word to its picture. هر کلمه را به شکلش وصل کن.

کَشتی

Car

تِرَن

Pigeon

ماشین

Ship

کَبوتَر

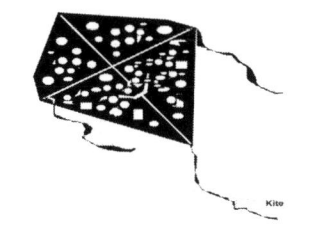

Kite

بادبادَک

Train

Read the word for each picture and
write the letters in the puzzle.

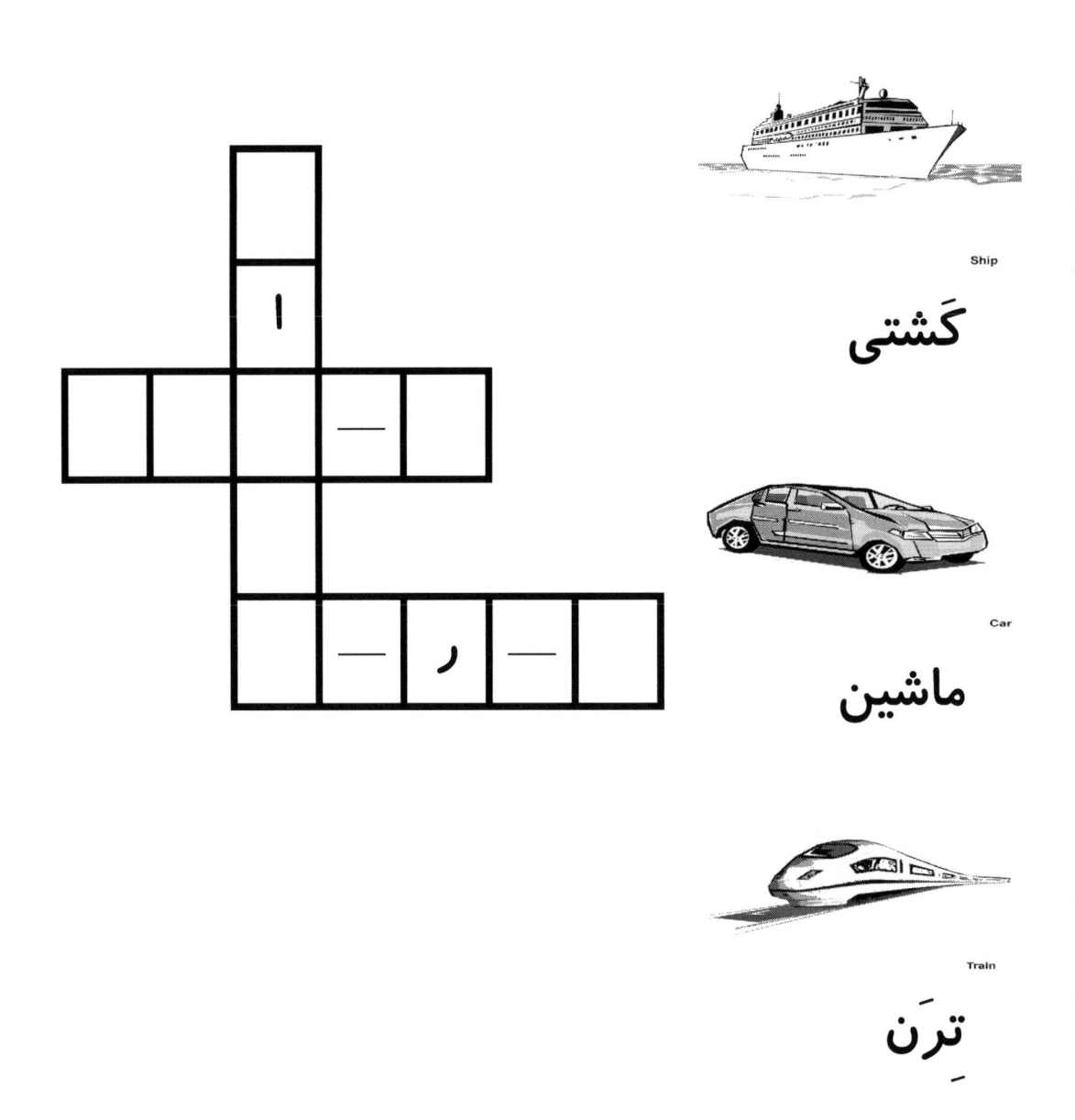

Ship

کَشتی

Car

ماشین

Train

تِرَن

۵۲

Find the word below in the puzzle.

کَشتی

و	ا	ض	ب	ل	ذِ	ج
د	ا	تِ	ل	ز	ا	ه
ش	ی	تِ	ش	کَ	ش	ا
ت	ی	ی	ا	د	ا	تِ
ف	ط	دُ	ه	رَ	ش	کَ

Look at this picture and write its name
under it.

به این شکل نگاه کن و اسمش را زیر آن
بنویس.

Train

_____

صداهای هر کلمه را بنویس.

__ + __ + __ + __ + __ = تِرَن

__ + __ + __ + __ + __ = کَشتی

__ + __ + __ + __ + __ = ماشین

Read the word below and draw a picture of it.

ماشین

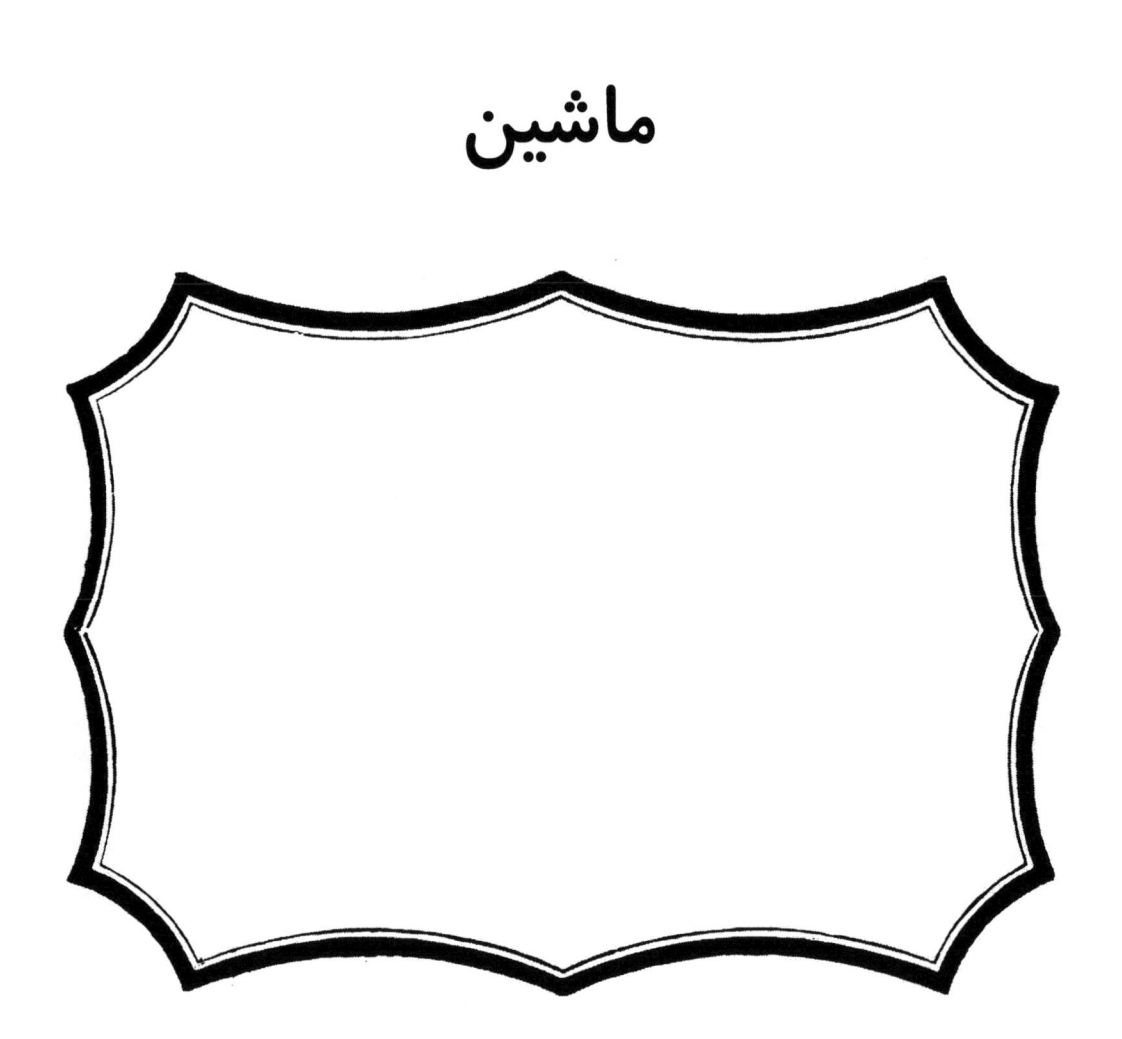

Exercise 8

كتاب

(ke. taab)

كراوات

(ke. raa. vaat)

مداد

(me. daad)

Read the word for each picture and
write the letters in their places.

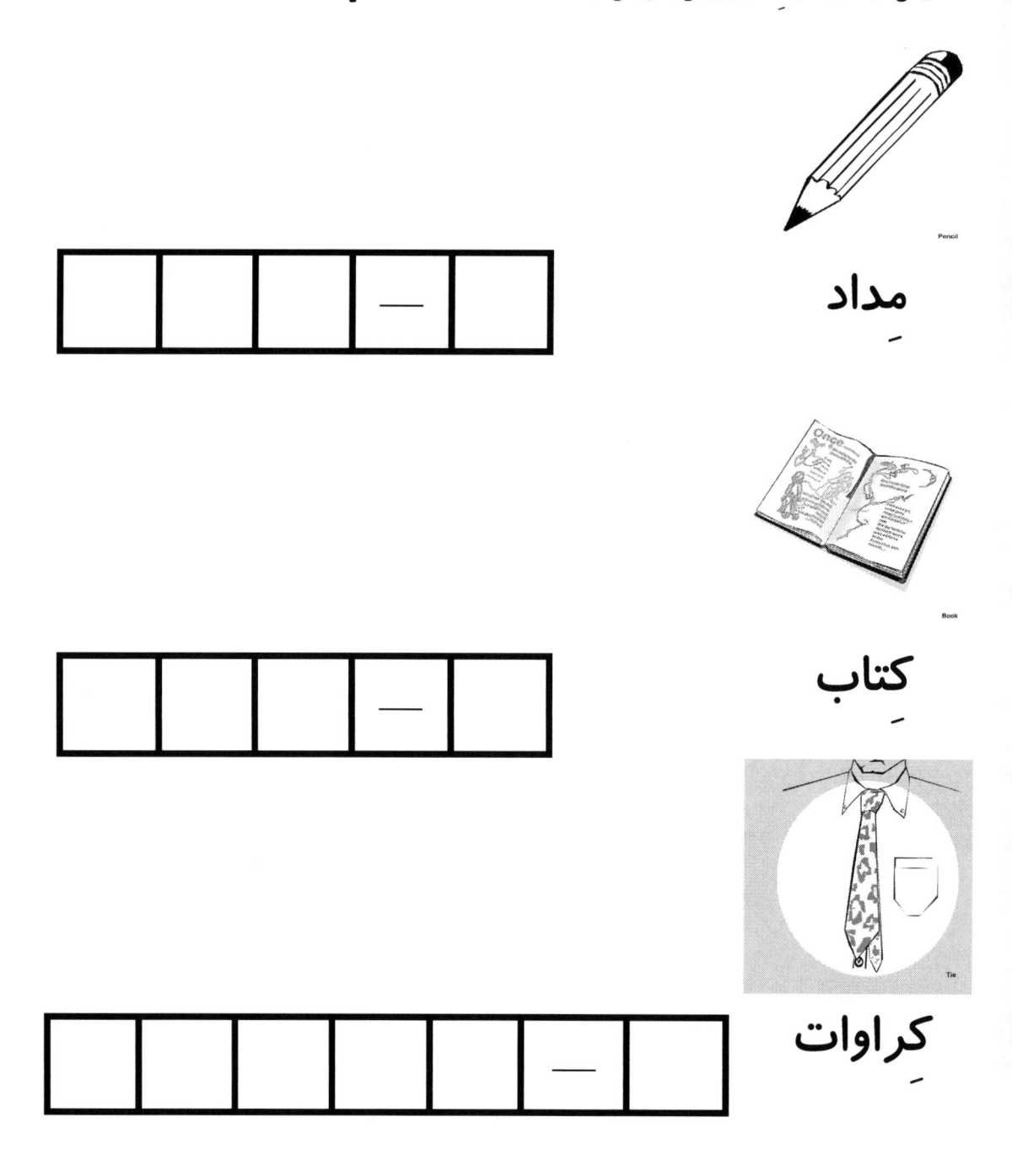

مِداد

کِتاب

کِراوات

Connect each word to its picture.

کِتاب

کَشتی

مِداد

تِرَن

کِراوات

Read the word for each picture and write the letters in the puzzle.

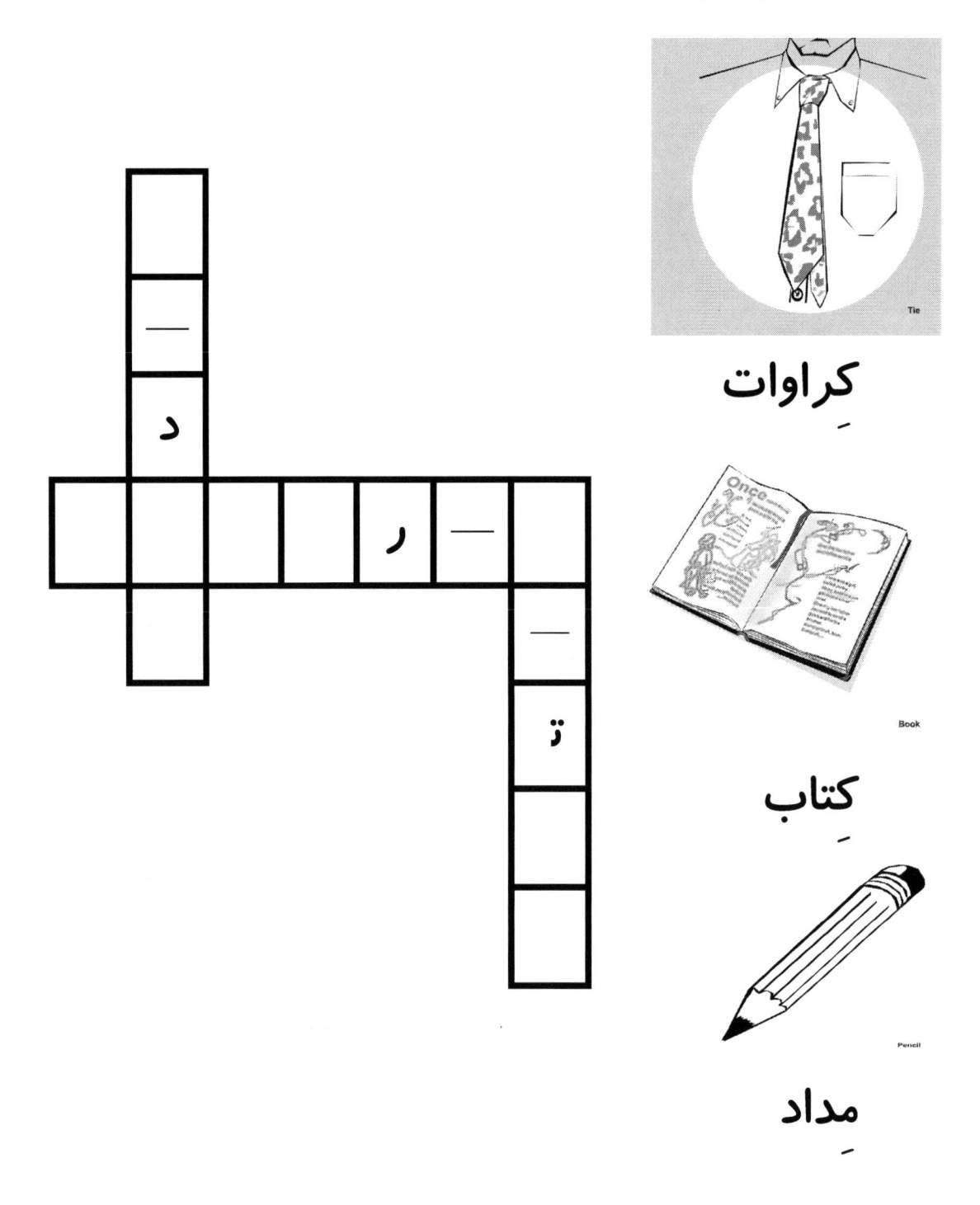

کِراوات

کِتاب

مِداد

Find the word below in the puzzle. كلمه زير را در جدول پيدا كن.

كِتاب

م	کِ	و	ا	ه	ر
ش	تَ	کُ	ه	تَ	ن
مـ	ا	ل	ر	کَ	ا
س	ب	يـ	گ	د	ز
ش	ا	کُ	ر	تَ	ل

Look at this picture and write its name under it.

به این شکل نگاه کن و اسمش را زیر آن بنویس.

Tie

_____

Write the letters for each word.   صداهای هر کلمه را بنویس.

__ + __ + __ + __ + __ = کِتاب

__ + __ + __ + __ + __ = مِداد

__ + __ + __ + __ + __ + __ + __ = کِراوات

Read the word below and draw a picture of it.

مِداد

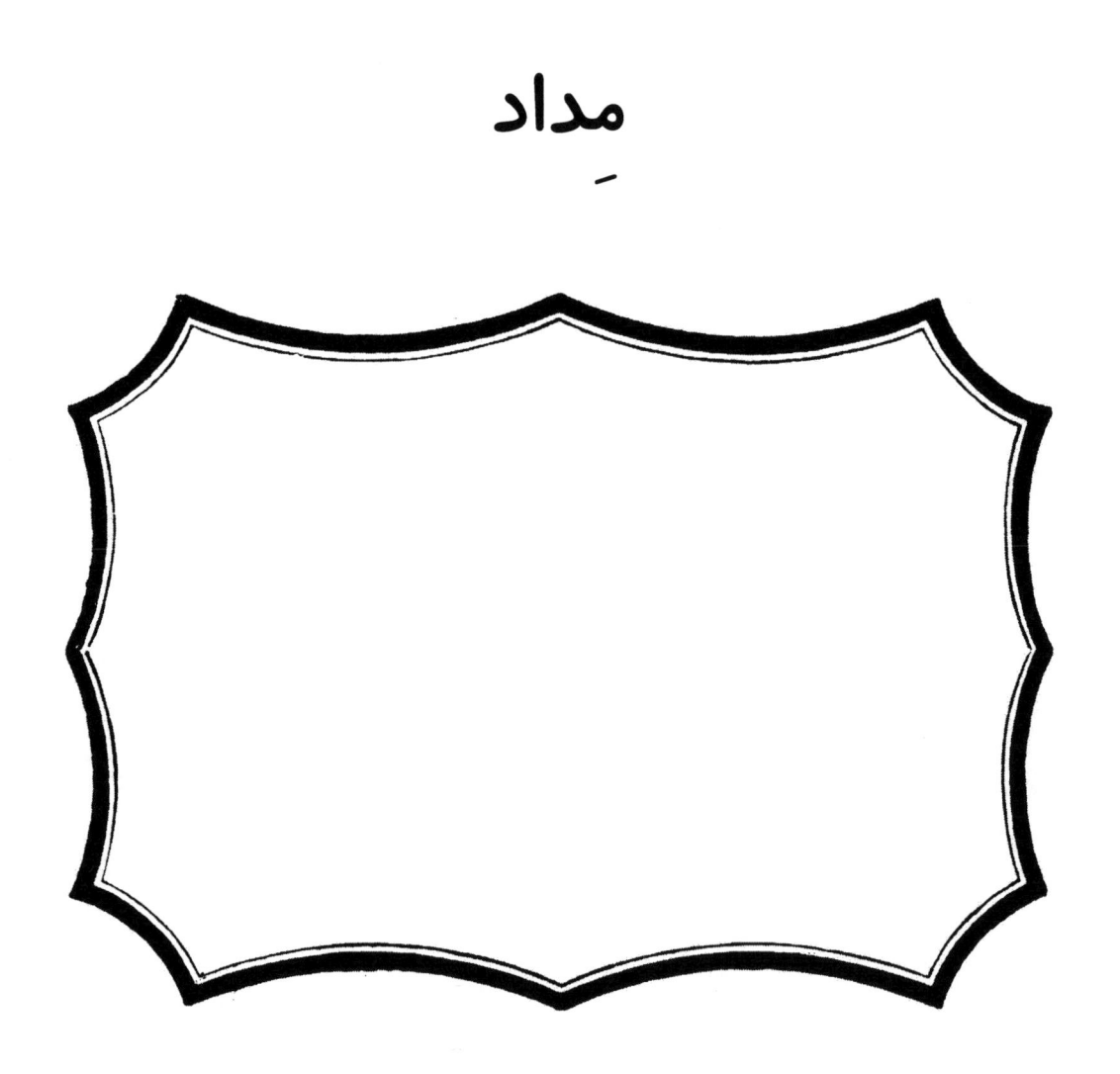

Exercise 9   ۹ تمرین

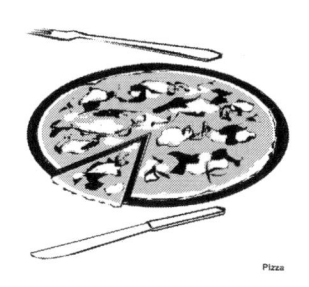

پیتزا

(peet. zaa)

بَبر

(babr)

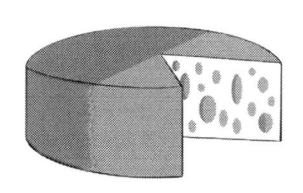

پَنیر

(pa. neer)

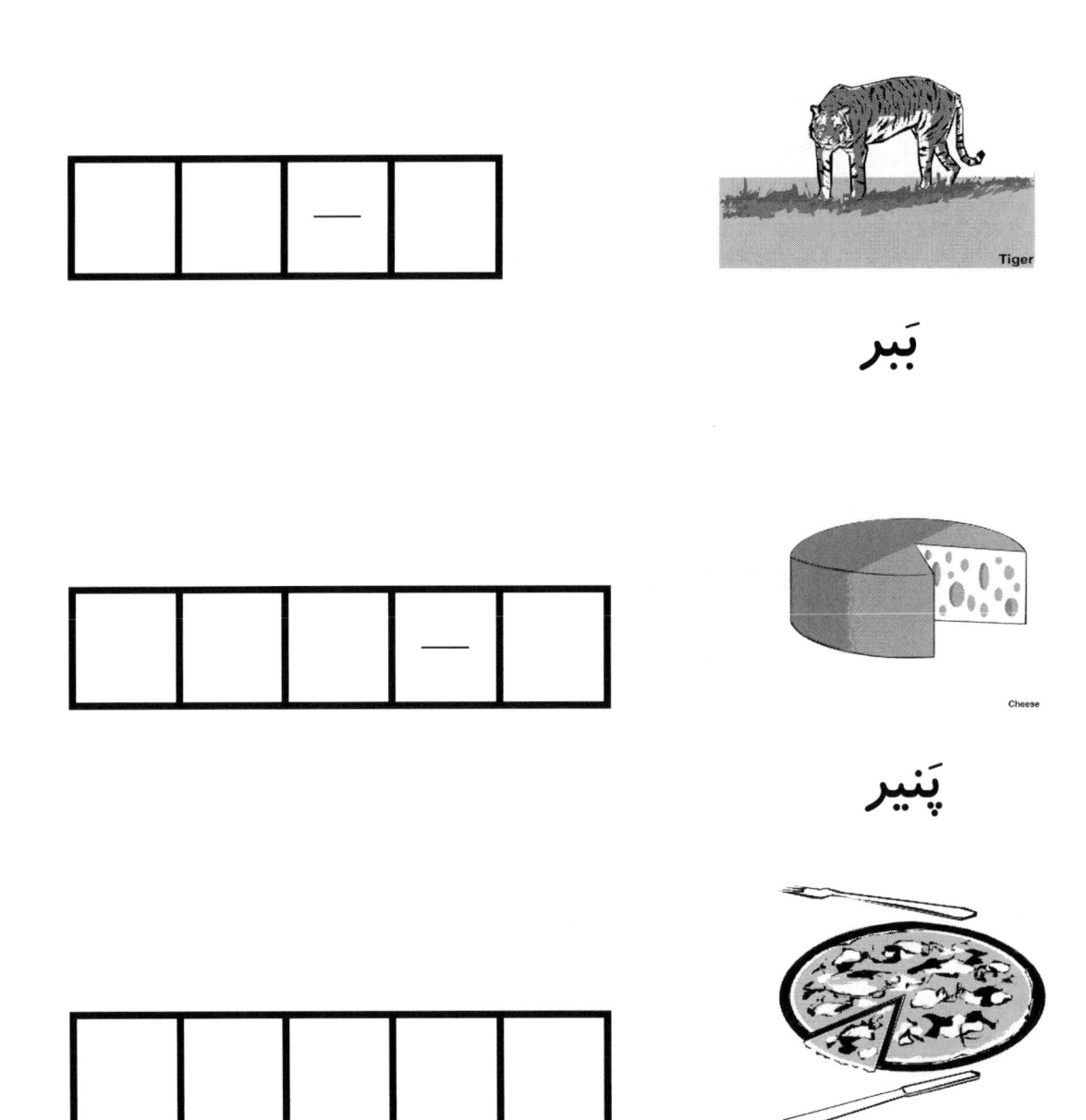

Read the word for each picture and write the letters in their places.

با کمک شکل ها، هر کلمه را بخوان و صداهایش را در جدولِ روبرویش بنویس.

Tiger

بَبر

Cheese

پَنیر

Pizza

پیتزا

Connect each word to its picture. هر کلمه را به شکلش وصل کن.

Tiger

پَنیر

Book

مِداد

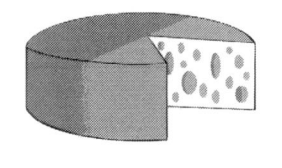

Cheese

بَبر

Pencil

پیتزا

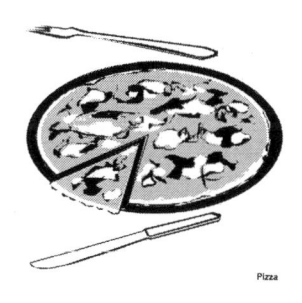

Pizza

کِتاب

Read the word for each picture and
write the letters in the puzzle.

با کمک شکل ها، هر کلمه را بخوان و جایش را در جدول پیدا کن.

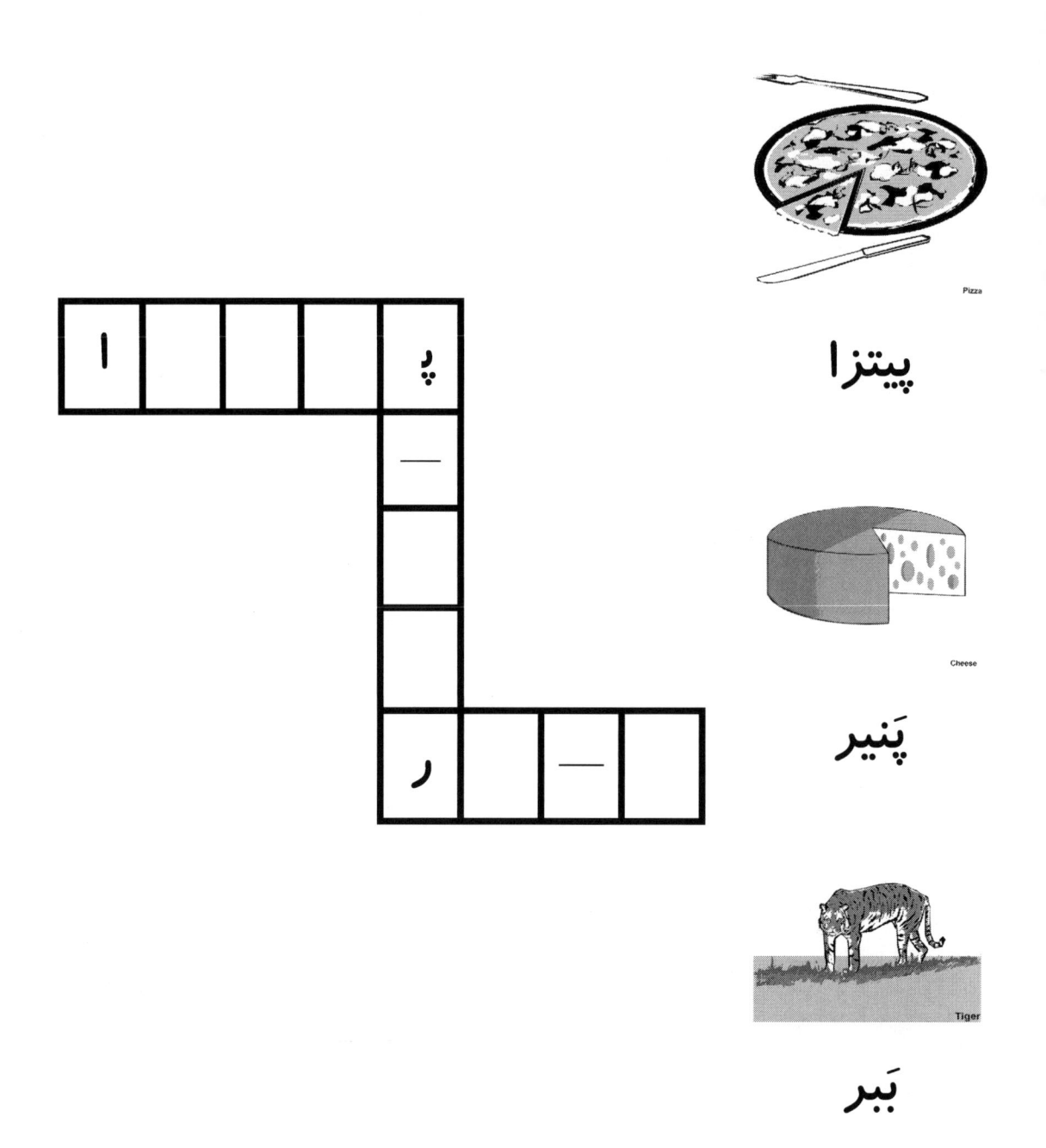

پیتزا

پَنیر

بَبر

بَبر

ب	ه	و	ر	ه	ا	تُ
ا	ر	ت	م	ا	ت	بِ
ک	سـ	بَ	ا	ذ	و	م
و	ه	ر	بِ	بَ	ر	ک
ن	م	ز	تِ	گ	ت	ا

Look at this picture and write its name under it.

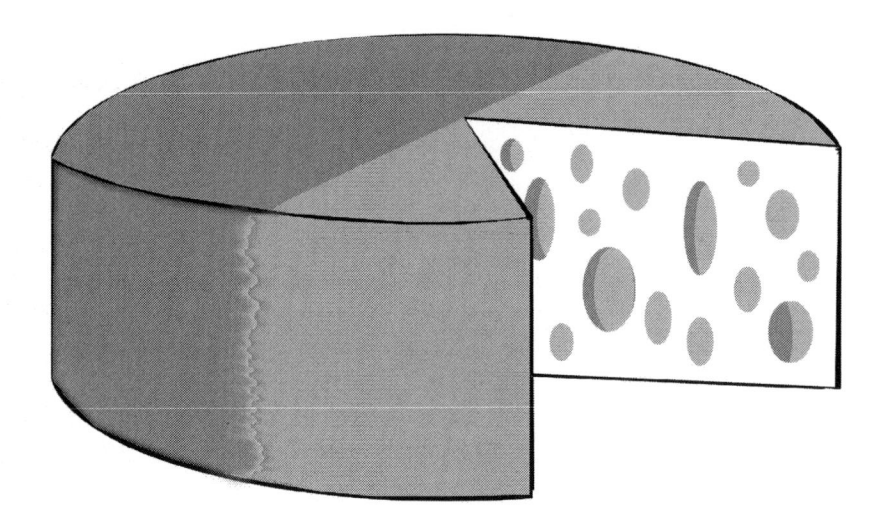

Cheese

_____

صداهای هر کلمه را بنویس.

__ + __ + __ + __ = بَبر

__ + __ + __ + __ + __ = پَنیر

__ + __ + __ + __ + __ = پیتزا

Read the word below and draw a picture of it.

کلمه زیر را بخوان و شکلش را بکش.

پیتزا

Exercise 10   ۱۰ تمرین

Cat

گُربه

(gor. be)

Butterfly

پَروانه

(par. vaa. ne)

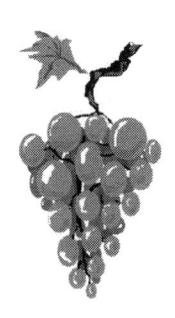

Grapes

اَنگور

(an. goor)

Read the word for each picture and
write the letters in their places.

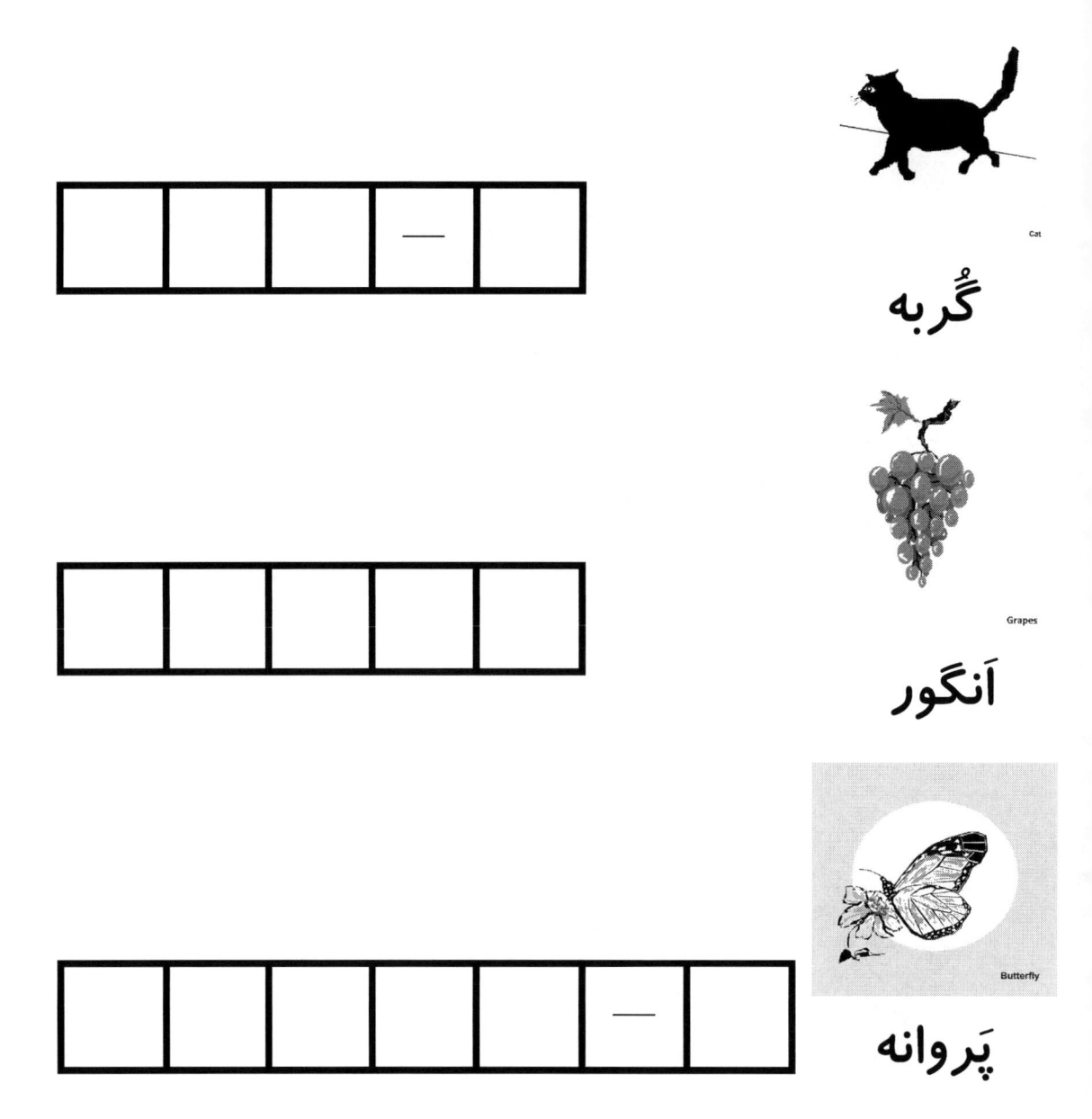

Cat

گُربه

Grapes

اَنگور

Butterfly

پَروانه

Connect each word to its picture.   هر کلمه را به شکلش وصل کن.

گُربه

اَنگور

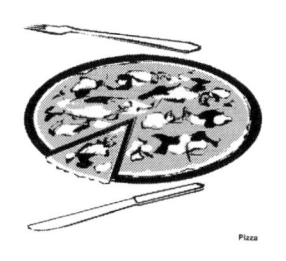

بَبر

پَروانه

پیتزا

Read the word for each picture and
write the letters in the puzzle.

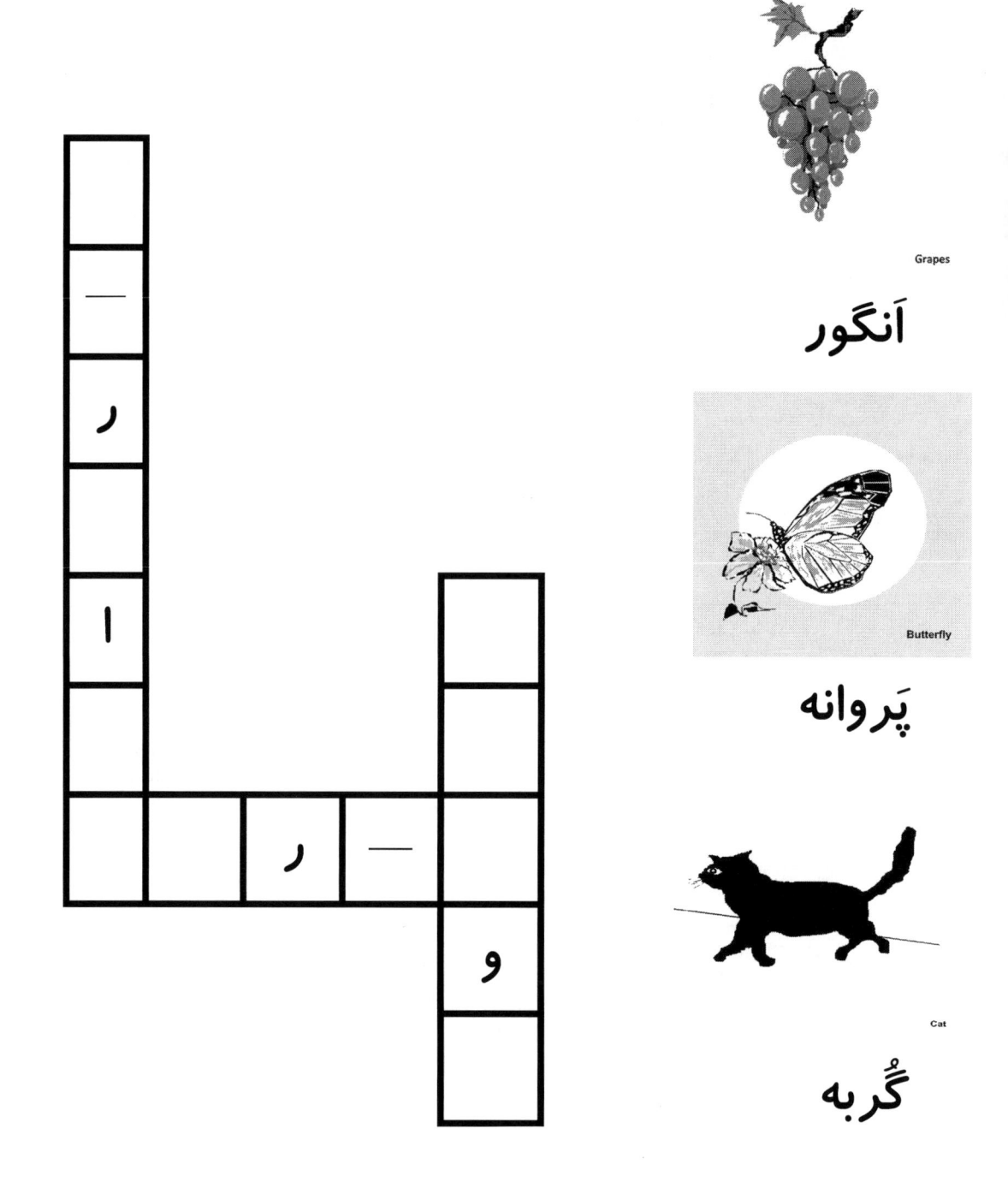

Grapes

اَنگور

Butterfly

پَروانه

Cat

گُربه

۷۶

Find the word below in the puzzle. كلمه زير را در جدول پيدا كن.

پَروانه

ه	ز	ا	و	ر	پَ
پ	د	ن	يـ	س	ا
و	ز	م	ک	ا	پَ
ه	ن	ى	يـ	م	و
ع	د	ذ	يـ	ش	ا

Look at this picture and write its name under it.

Grapes

_____

Write the letters for each word.

صداهای هر کلمه را بنویس.

گُربه= __ + __ + __ + __ + __

اَنگور= __ + __ + __ + __ + __

پَروانه= __ + __ + __ + __ + __ + __ + __

Read the word below and draw a picture of it.

گُربه

Exercise 11   ۱۱ تمرین

كيف

(keef)

كَفش

(kafsh)

نيمكَت

(neem. kat)

Read the word for each picture and
write the letters in their places.

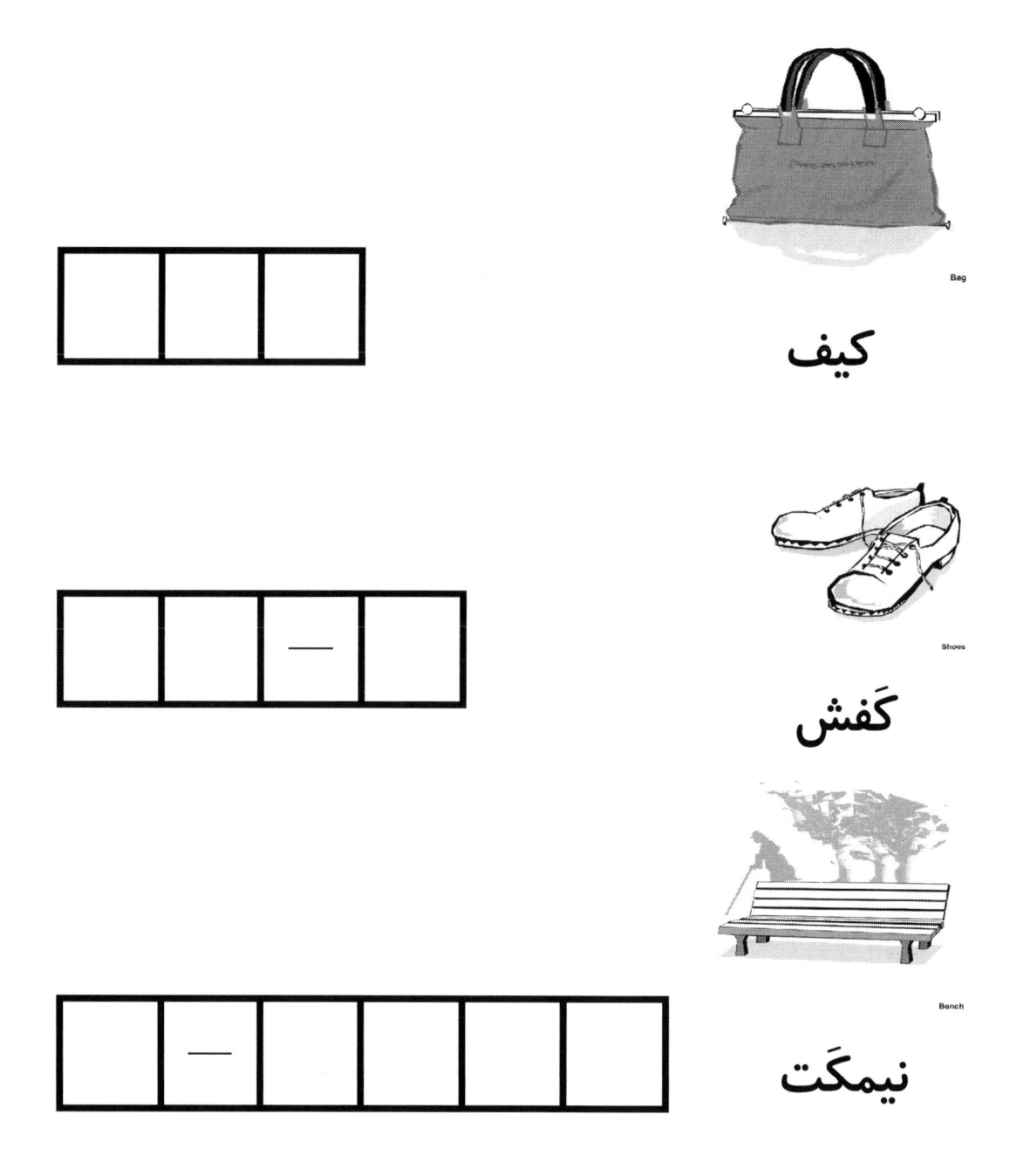

Bag

کیف

Shoes

کَفش

Bench

نیمکَت

Connect each word to its picture.

هر کلمه را به شکلش وصل کن.

Bag

کَفش

Grapes

گُربه

Shoes

نیمکَت

Cat

کیف

Bench

اَنگور

Read the word for each picture and
write the letters in the puzzle.

با کمک شکل ها، هر کلمه را بخوان و
جایش را در جدول پیدا کن.

Bench

نیمکَت

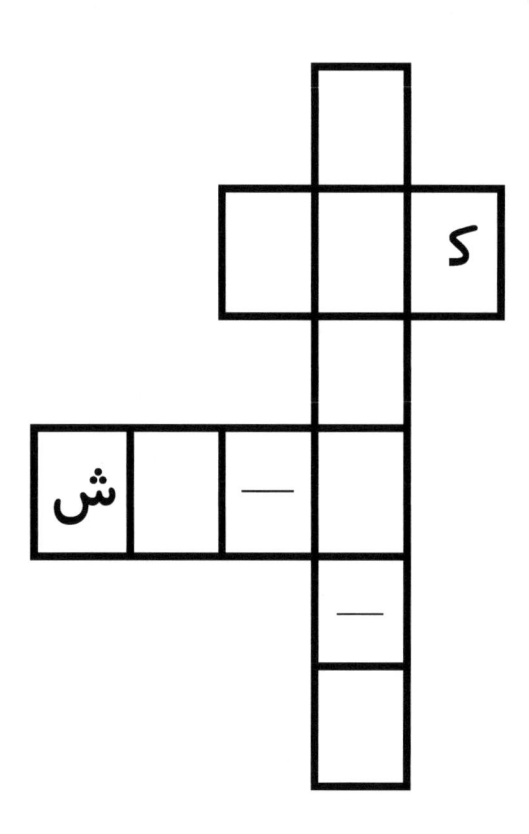

Shoes

کَفش

Bag

کیف

Find the word below in the puzzle.

نیمکَت

ن	ب	د	ذِ	ز	و	ل
ش	ا	و	یِ	ل	ا	گَ
تَ	ذِ	ا	م	بِ	گَ	ا
بِ	م	ر	گَ	و	ه	خ
ک	ا	ل	ت	کِ	ا	گُ

Look at this picture and write its name under it.

Bag

_____

Write the letters for each word.

صداهای هر کلمه را بنویس.

کیف = __ + __ + __

کَفش = __ + __ + __ + __

نیمکَت = __ + __ + __ + __ + __ + __

Read the word below and draw a picture of it.

کلمه زیر را بخوان و شکلش را بکش.

کَفش

Exercise 12   تمرين ۱۲

خُروس

(ǩo. roos)

ساختمان

(saaǩ. tē. maan)

سیب

(seeb)

Read the word for each picture and write the letters in their places.

با کمک شکل ها، هر کلمه را بخوان و صداهایش را در جدولِ روبرویش بنویس.

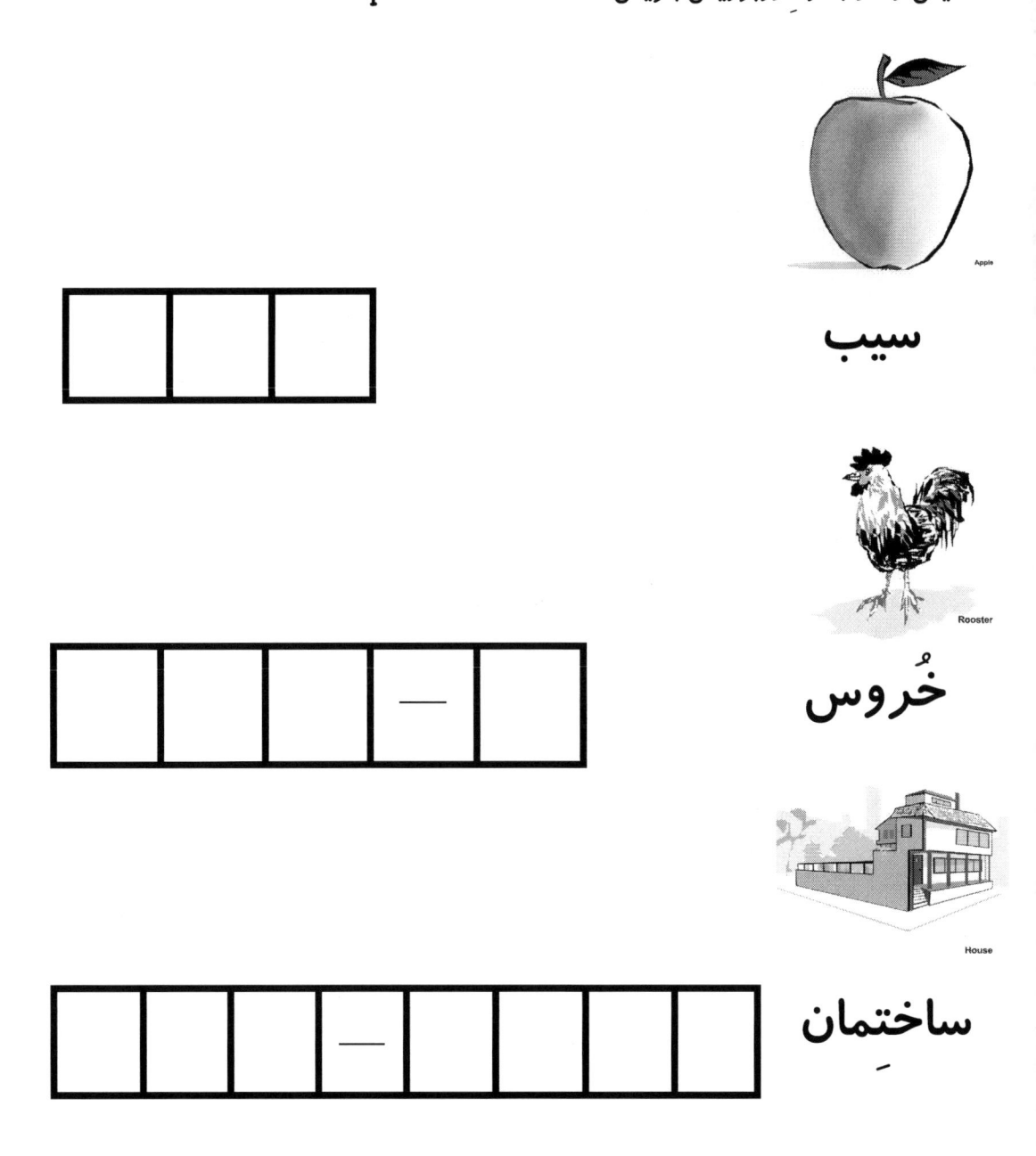

سیب

خُروس

ساخِتمانِ

Connect each word to its picture.

Rooster

ساختِمان

Bag

کَفش

House

سیب

Shoes

کیف

Apple

خُروس

۹۱

Read the word for each picture and write the letters in the puzzle.

با کمک شکل ها، هر کلمه را بخوان و جایش را در جدول پیدا کن.

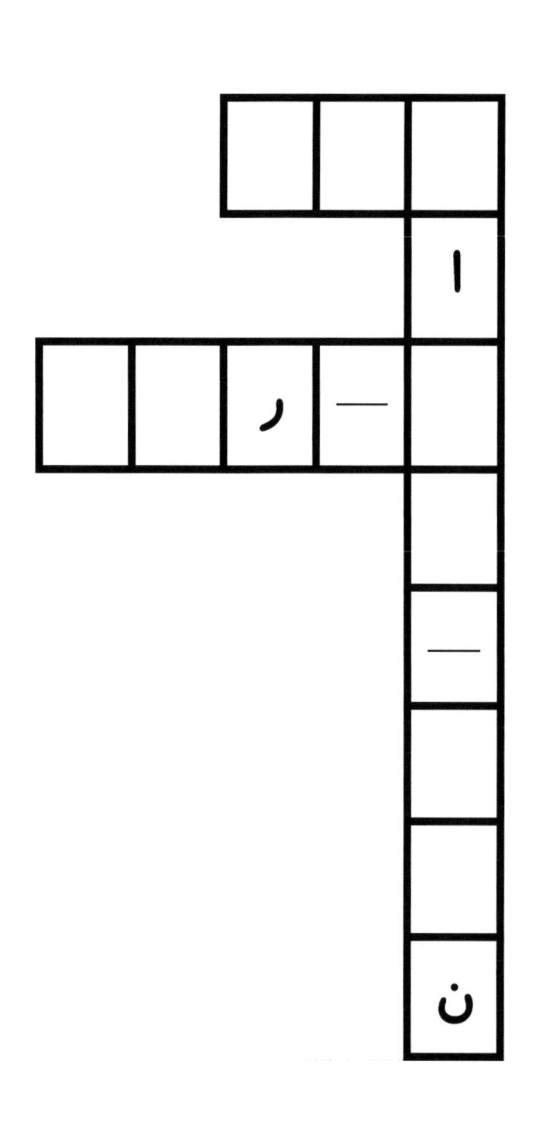

Rooster

خُروس

House

ساختمان

Apple

سیب

Find the word below in the puzzle. كلمه زير را در جدول پيدا كن.

خُروس

ف	ه	ل	و	نُ خ	س
و	زِ	اُ	ذ	ل	ر	م
ه	ل	خُ	ن	س	و	ا
ل	اِ	ی	گ	ن	س	ر
پ	و	ص	ب	ذ	ر	اَ

Look at this picture and write its name under it.

Apple

_____

Write the letters for each word. صداهای هر کلمه را بنویس.

سیب= ﹍ + ﹍ + ﹍

خُروس= ﹍ + ﹍ + ﹍ + ﹍ + ﹍

ساختمان= ﹍+﹍+﹍+﹍+﹍+﹍+﹍+﹍

ساختِمان

Exercise 13 ١٣ تمرين

Kettle

قوری

(ğoo. ree)

Plate

بُشقاب

(bosh. ğaab)

Spoon

قاشُق

(ğaa. shoğ)

با کمک شکل ها، هر کلمه را بخوان و
صداهایش را در جدولِ روبرویش بنویس.

Read the word for each picture and write the letters in their places.

Kettle

قوری

Spoon

قاشُق

Plate

بُشقاب

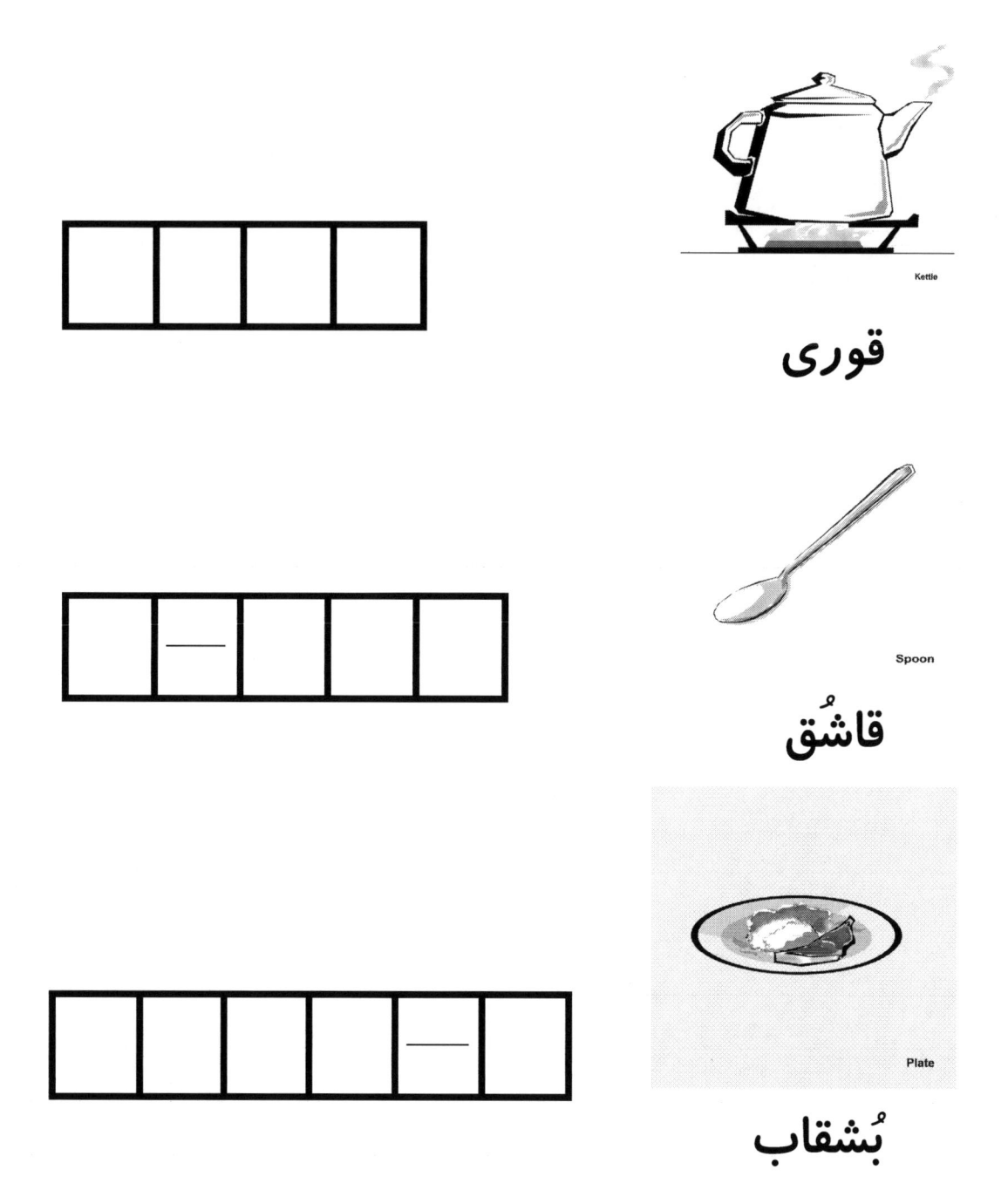

Connect each word to its picture.

هر کلمه را به شکلش وصل کن.

Plate

ساختِمان

House

قاشُق

Kettle

کیف

بُشقاب

Bag

قوری

Spoon

٩٩

Read the word for each picture and
write the letters in the puzzle.

با کمک شکل ها، هر کلمه را بخوان و
جایش را در جدول پیدا کن.

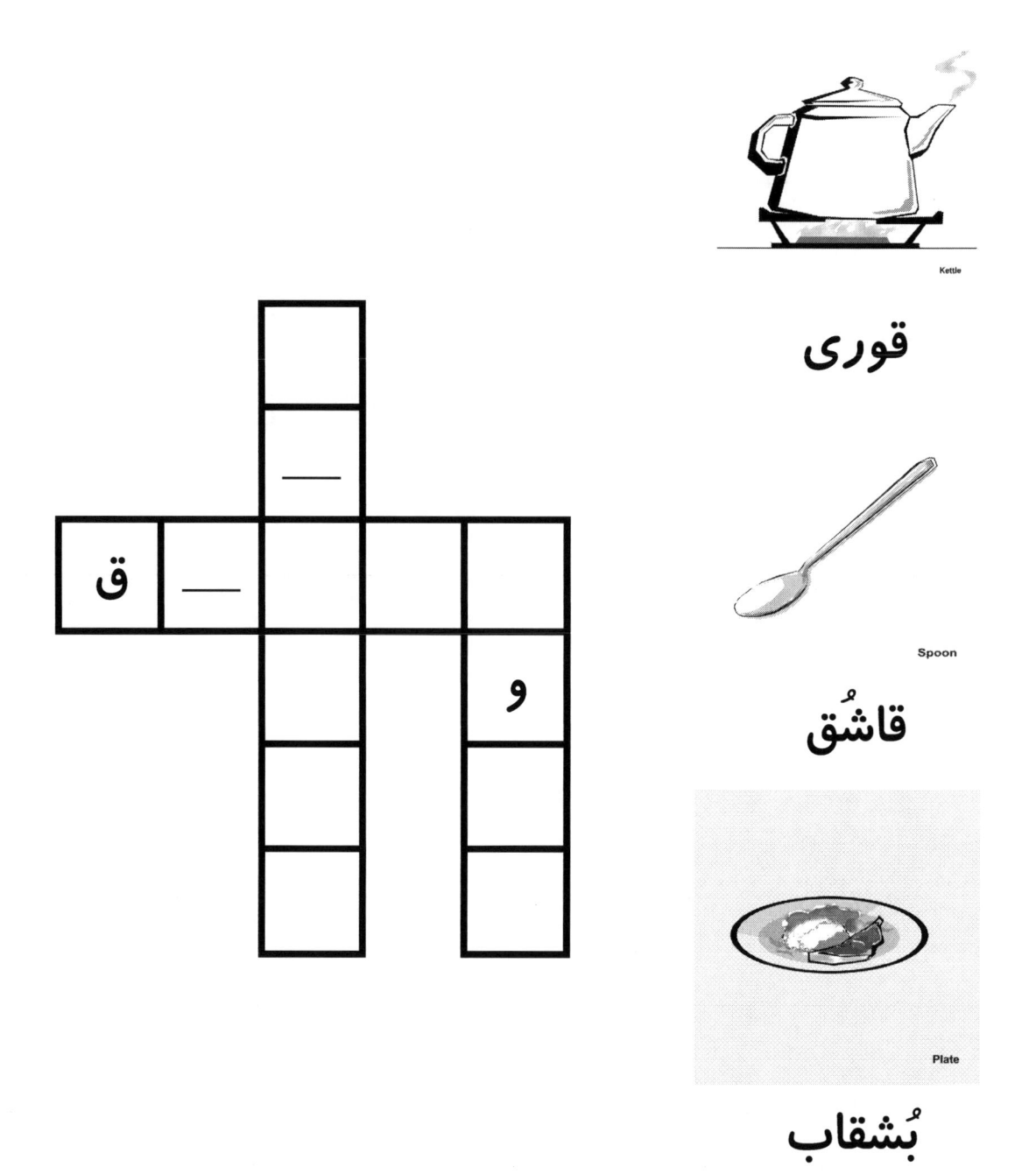

قوری

قاشُق

بُشقاب

قاشُق

ق	ا	ث	و	ل	ک
ا	چ	ه	ف	ا	چ
شُ	پ	ق	شُ	و	ا
ق	بِ	ا	ز	ر	م
س	پِ	ض	ی	ذ	و

Look at this picture and write its name under it.

به این شکل نگاه کن و اسمش را زیر آن بنویس.

Kettle

_____

Write the letters for each word. صداهای هر کلمه را بنویس.

قاشُق = __ + __ + __ + __ + __

قوری = __ + __ + __ + __

بُشقاب = __ + __ + __ + __ + __ + __

Read the word below and draw a picture of it.

بُشقاب

Exercise 14

Cherries

گیلاس

(gee. laas)

Socks

جوراب

(joo. raab)

Orange

پُرتقال

(por. te. ğaal)

Read the word for each picture and
write the letters in their places.

با کمک شکل ها، هر کلمه را بخوان و
صداهایش را در جدولِ روبرویش بنویس.

Socks

جوراب

Cherries

گیلاس

Orange

پُرتِقال

Connect each word to its picture. هر کلمه را به شکلش وصل کن.

Orange

جوراب

Spoon

قوری

Cherries

پُرتِقال

Kettle

قاشُق

Socks

گیلاس

Read the word for each picture and
write the letters in the puzzle.

با کمک شکل ها، هر کلمه را بخوان و
جایش را در جدول پیدا کن.

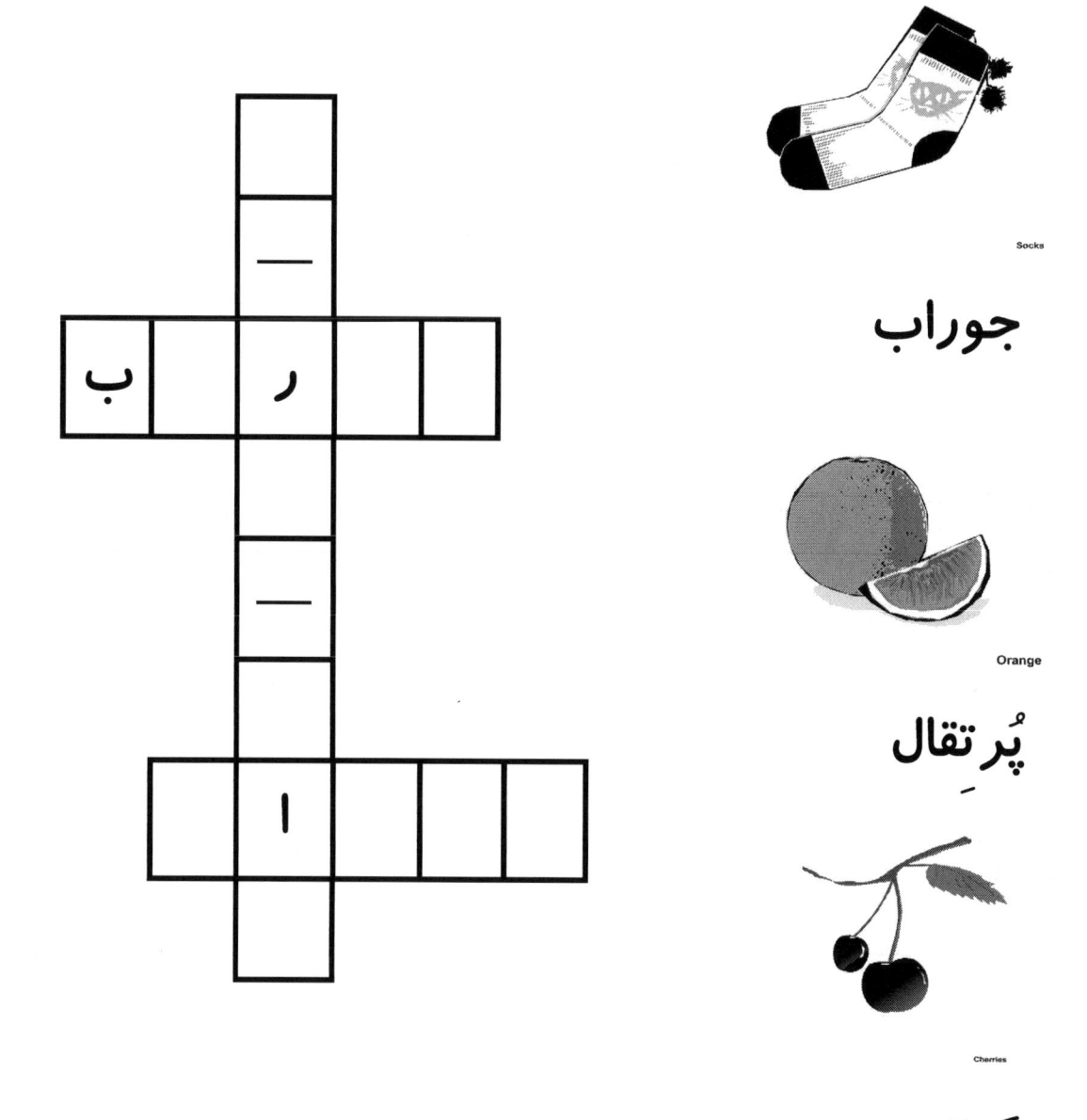

Socks

جوراب

Orange

پُرتِقال

Cherries

گیلاس

Find the word below in the puzzle.

کلمه زیر را در جدول پیدا کن.

جوراب

س	ج	ن	و	ل	ج	ف
م	و	ل	ذ	اُ	ز	و
ا	ر	و	ن	ف	ل	ه
ت	ا	ب	گ	ی	اِ	ل
اَ	ب	ذ	ب	ص	و	پ

Orange

گیلاس = __ + __ + __ + __ + __

جوراب = __ + __ + __ + __ + __

پُرِتقال = __ + __ + __ + __ + __ + __ + __ + __

Read the word below and draw a picture of it.

گیلاس

Exercise 15 تمرین ۱۵

پالتو

(paal. to)

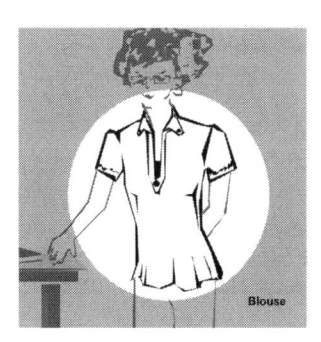

بُلوز

(bo. looz)

اُتوبوس

(o. to. boos)

Read the word for each picture and
write the letters in their places.

با کمک شکل ها، هر کلمه را بخوان و
صداهایش را در جدولِ روبرویش بنویس.

بُلوز

Blouse

پالتو

Coat

اُتوبوس

Bus

۱۱۴

Connect each word to its picture.

Bus

جوراب

Socke

بُلوز

Coat

اُتوبوس

Orange

پالتو

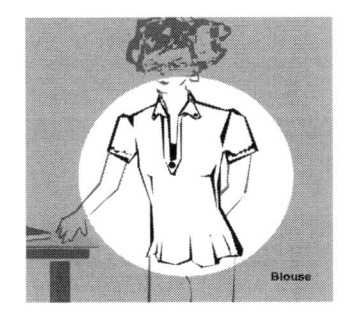

Blouse

پُرِتقال

Read the word for each picture and write the letters in the puzzle.

با کمک شکل ها، هر کلمه را بخوان و جایش را در جدول پیدا کن.

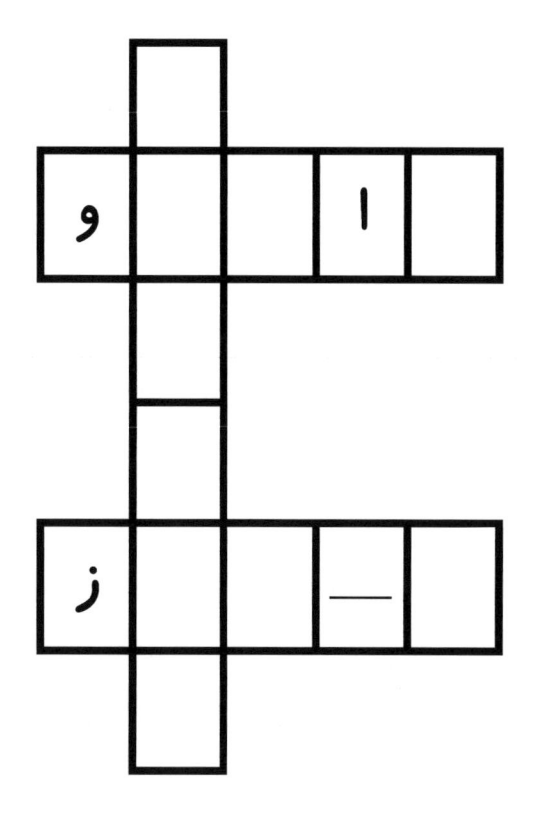

Bus

اُتوبوس

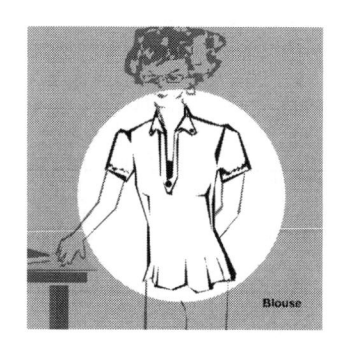

Blouse

بُلوز

Coat

پالتو

Find the word below in the puzzle. کلمه زیر را در جدول پیدا کن.

نَوروز

ن	ر	ا.و	ا.و.۱	۱
ت	و	ون	۱	م
هن	۱	و.و	م	ا.و.۱
وم	ن.و	۱	ون	ه
ج	ل	و	ظ	ح
ه	ک	ر	۱	ن

Look at this picture and write its name under it.

به این شکل نگاه کن و اسمش را زیر آن بنویس.

Coat

_____

Write the letters for each word.

بُلوز= __ + __ + __ + __ + __

پالتو= __ + __ + __ + __ + __

اُتوبوس= __ + __ + __ + __ + __ + __

Read the word below and draw a picture of it.

کلمه زیر را بخوان و شکلش را بکش.

Exercise 16 ١٦ تمرین

Plane

هَواپیما

(ha. vaa. pey. maa)

Hamburger

هَمبرگر

(ham. ber. ger)

Fox

روباه

(roo. baah)

Read the word for each picture and
write the letters in their places.

با کمک شکل ها، هر کلمه را بخوان و
صداهایش را در جدولِ روبرویش بنویس.

روباه

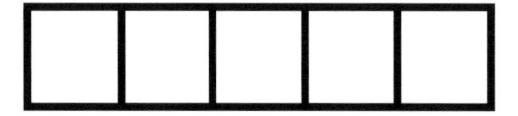

هَمبِرگِر

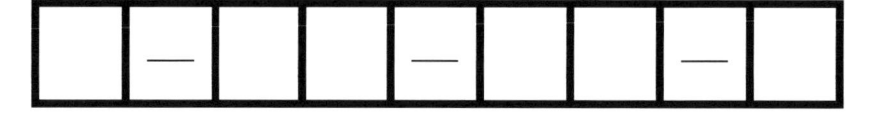

Plane

هَواپِیما

Connect each word to its picture.

اُتوبوس

روباه

هَمبِرگِر

هَواپِیما

پالتو

Read the word for each picture and write the letters in the puzzle.

به کمک شکل ها، هر کلمه را بخوان و جایش را در جدول پیدا کن.

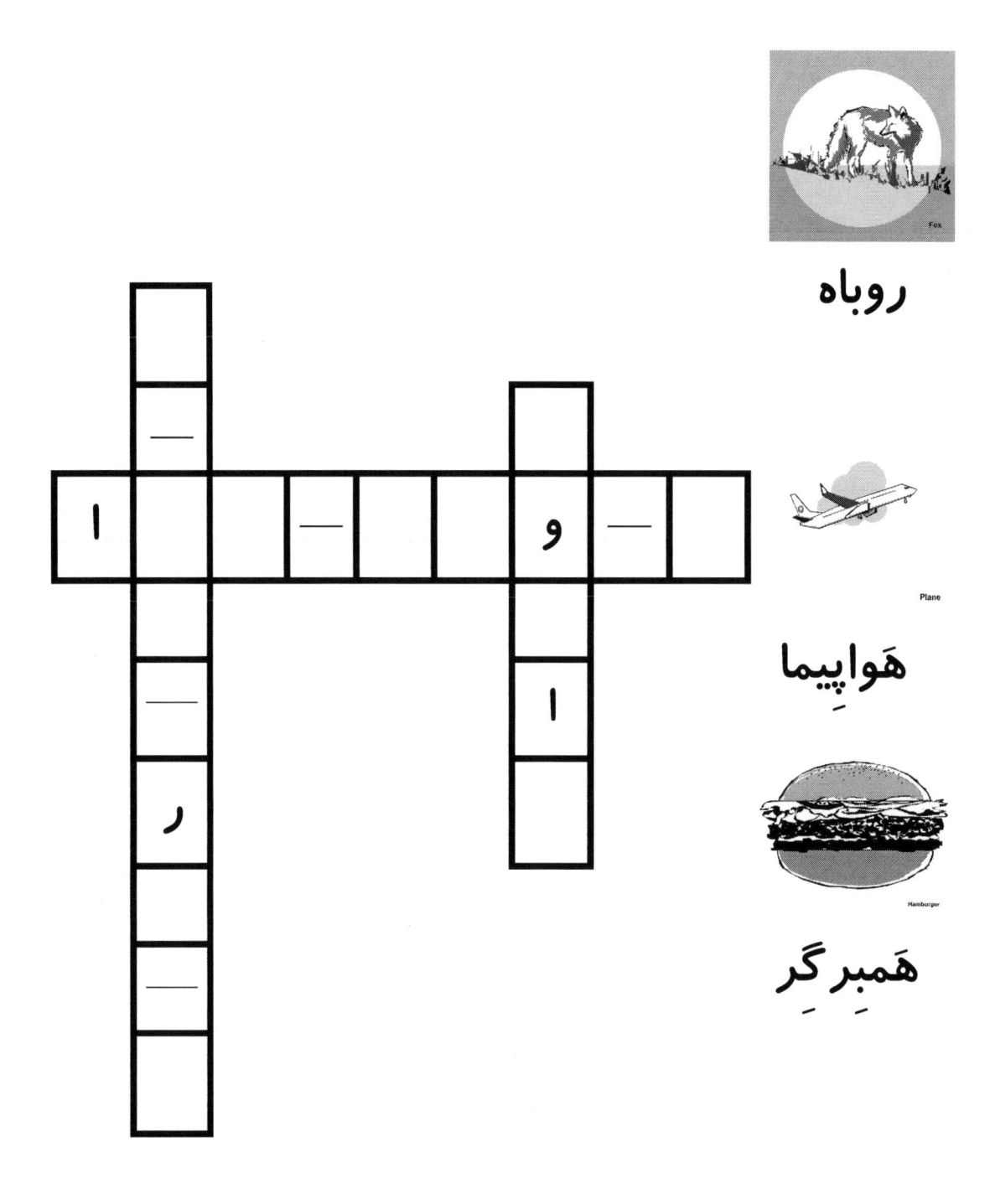

روباه

هَواپِیما

هَمبِرِگِر

Find the word below in the puzzle.

کلمه زیر را در جدول پیدا کن.

روباه

ب	ه	ا	ر	ه	ا	ت
ا	ر	ف	م	ا	ت	بِ
ک	س	بِ	ا	ذ	و	م
و	ه	ا	بِ	و	ر	ک
ن	م	ر	تِ	گ	ت	ا

Look at this picture and write its name under it.

به این شکل نگاه کن و اسمش را زیر آن بنویس.

Hamburger

روباه = ___ + ___ + ___ + ___ + ___

هَمبِرگِر = ___ + ___ + ___ + ___ + ___ + ___ + ___ + ___

هَواپِیما = ___ + ___ + ___ + ___ + ___ + ___ + ___ + ___

Read the word below and draw a picture of it.

کلمه زیر را بخوان و شکلش را بکش.

هَواپیما

Exercise 17   تمرین ۱۷

كُلاه

(ko. laah)

يَخچال

(yaک. chaal)

چَنگال

(chan. gaal)

Read the word for each picture and
write the letters in their places.

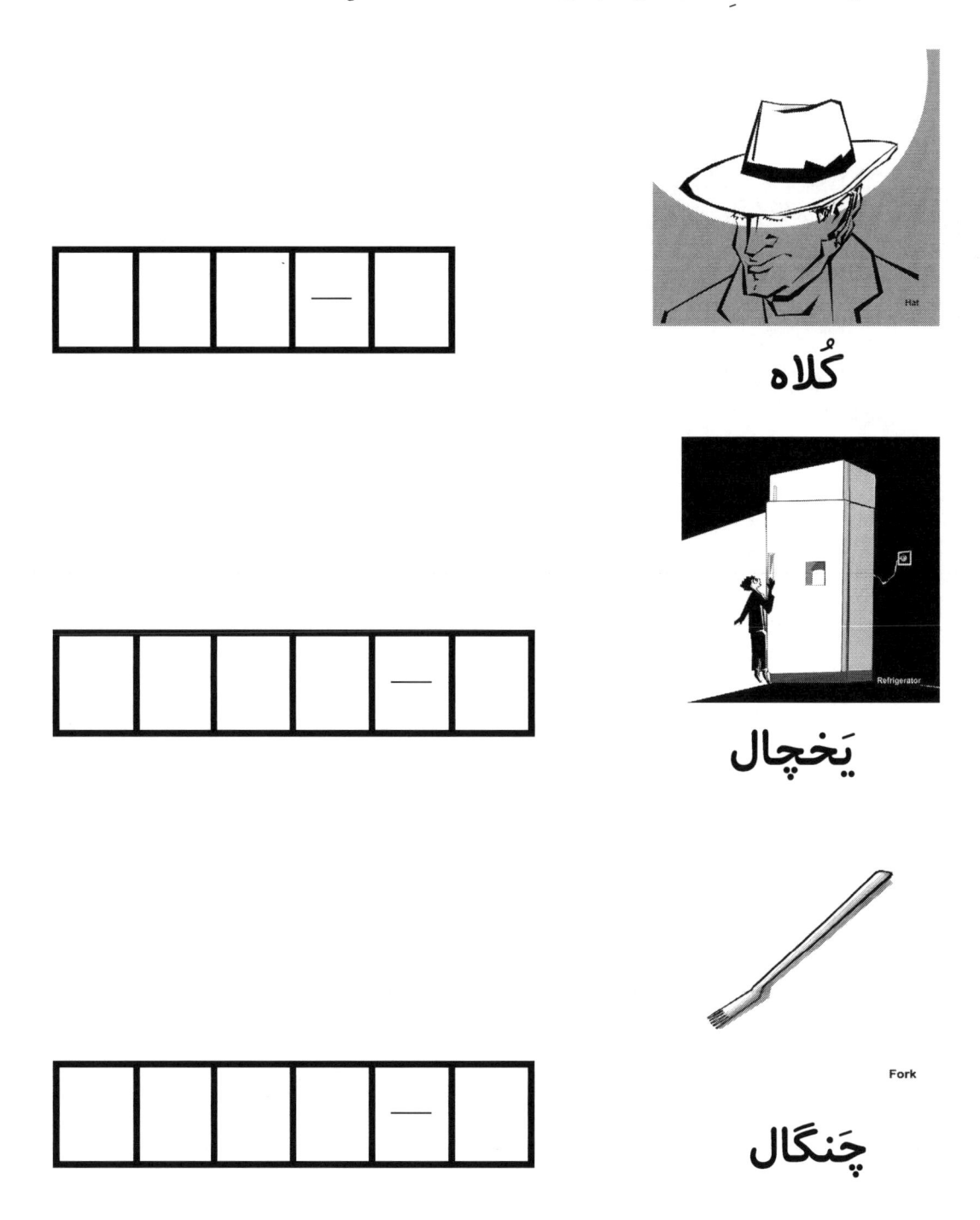

کُلاه

یَخچال

Fork

چَنگال

Connect each word to its picture. هر کلمه را به شکلش وصل کن.

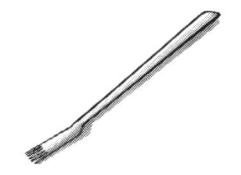

Fork

كُلاه

Hamburger

هَمبِرگِر

Hat

يَخچال

Plane

چَنگال

Refrigerator

هَواپِیما

Read the word for each picture and write the letters in the puzzle.

با کمک شکل ها، هر کلمه را بخوان و جایش را در جدول پیدا کن.

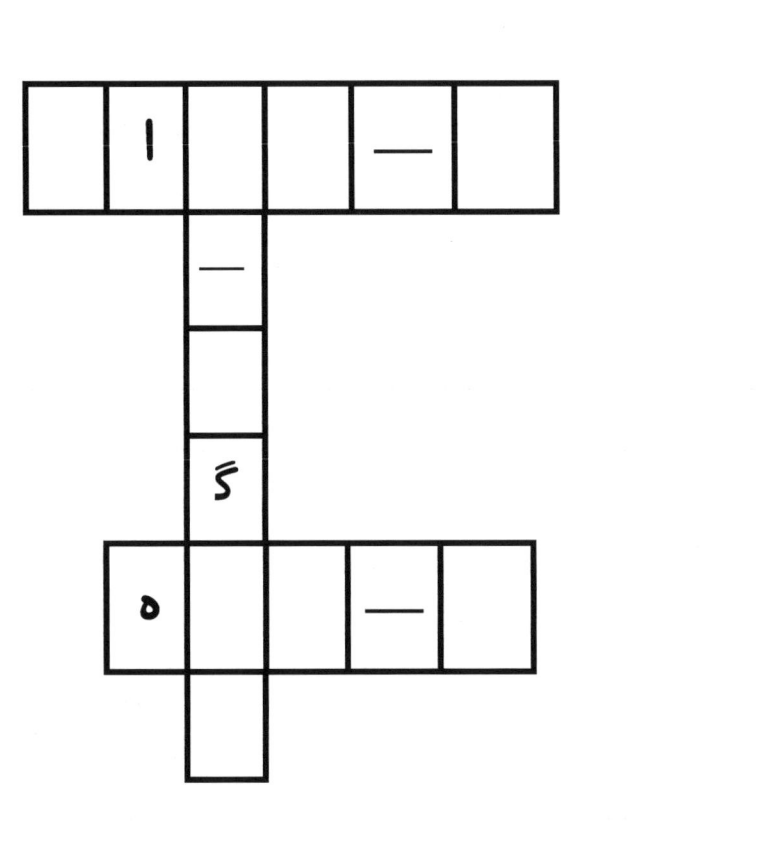

Fork

چَنگال

کُلاه

یَخچال

Find the word below in the puzzle.

کُلاه

چ	ژ	یِ	ف	ط	ز	ب
کِ	ل	و	ز	گَ	ا	د
ذ	پ	گُ	ل	ا	ه	ظ
ا	خ	ه	م	ی	سَ	ه
ه	ق	ح	ت	ا	ز	ی

Look at this picture and write its name under it.

به این شکل نگاه کن و اسمش را زیر آن بنویس.

Refrigerator

__ + __ + __ + __ + __ = کُلاه

__ + __ + __ + __ + __ + __ = یَخچال

__ + __ + __ + __ + __ + __ = چَنگال

Read the word below and draw a picture
of it.

کلمه زیر را بخوان و شکلش را
بکش.

چَنگال

Exercise 18 ١٨ تمرين

شَلوار

(shal. vaar)

Bicycle

دوچَرخه

(do. char. ǩe)

Dragon

اژدها

(ež. dé. hɑa)

Read the word for each picture and
write the letters in their places.

با کمک شکل ها، هر کلمه را بخوان و
صداهایش را در جدولِ روبرویش بنویس.

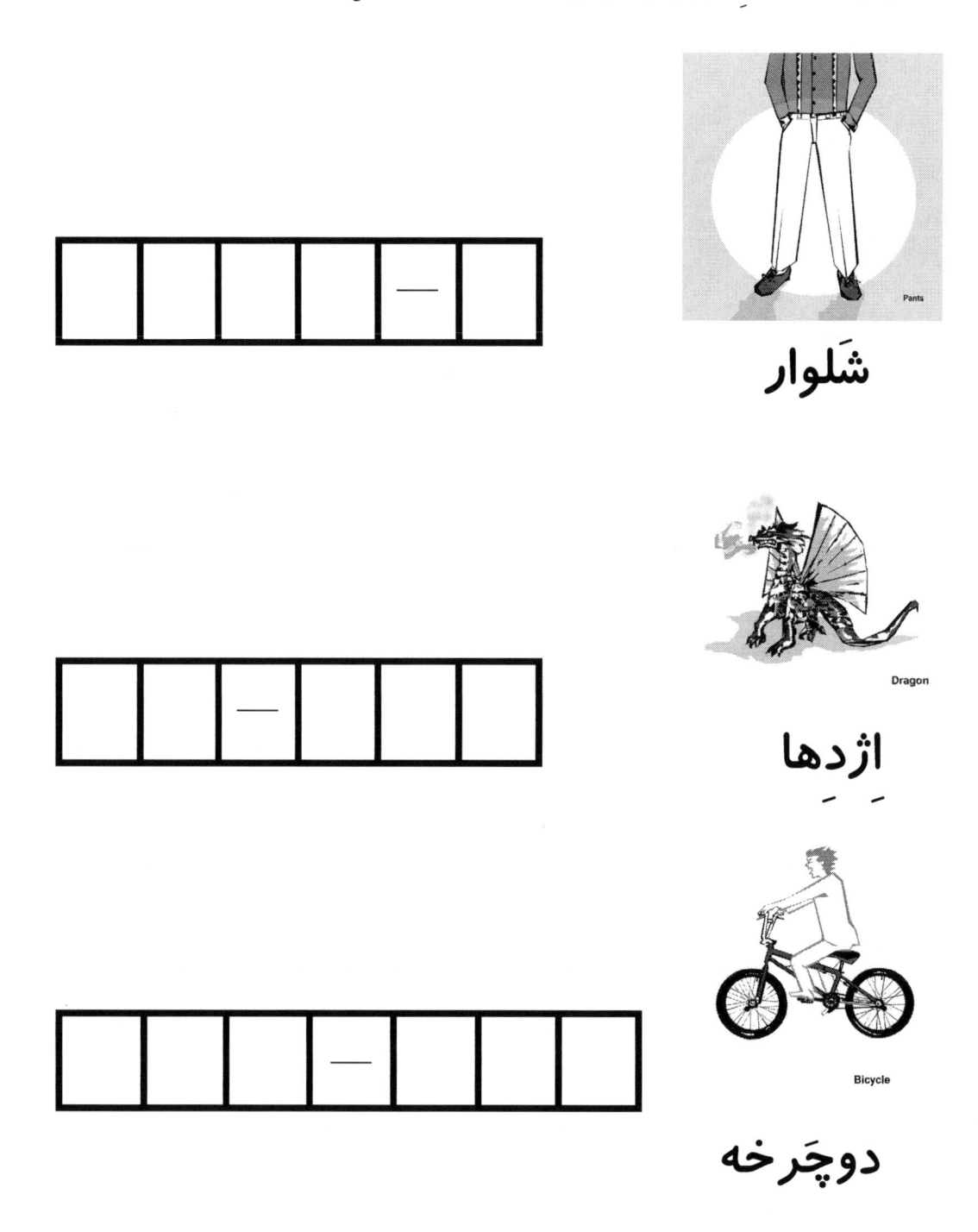

شَلوار

Pants

Dragon

اژدها

Bicycle

دوچَرخه

Connect each word to its picture.

Bicycle

اِژدِها

Refrigerator

دوچَرخه

Pants

کُلاه

Hat

یَخچال

شَلوار

Dragon

Read the word for each picture and
write the letters in the puzzle.

با کمک شکل ها، هر کلمه را بخوان و
جایش را در جدول پیدا کن.

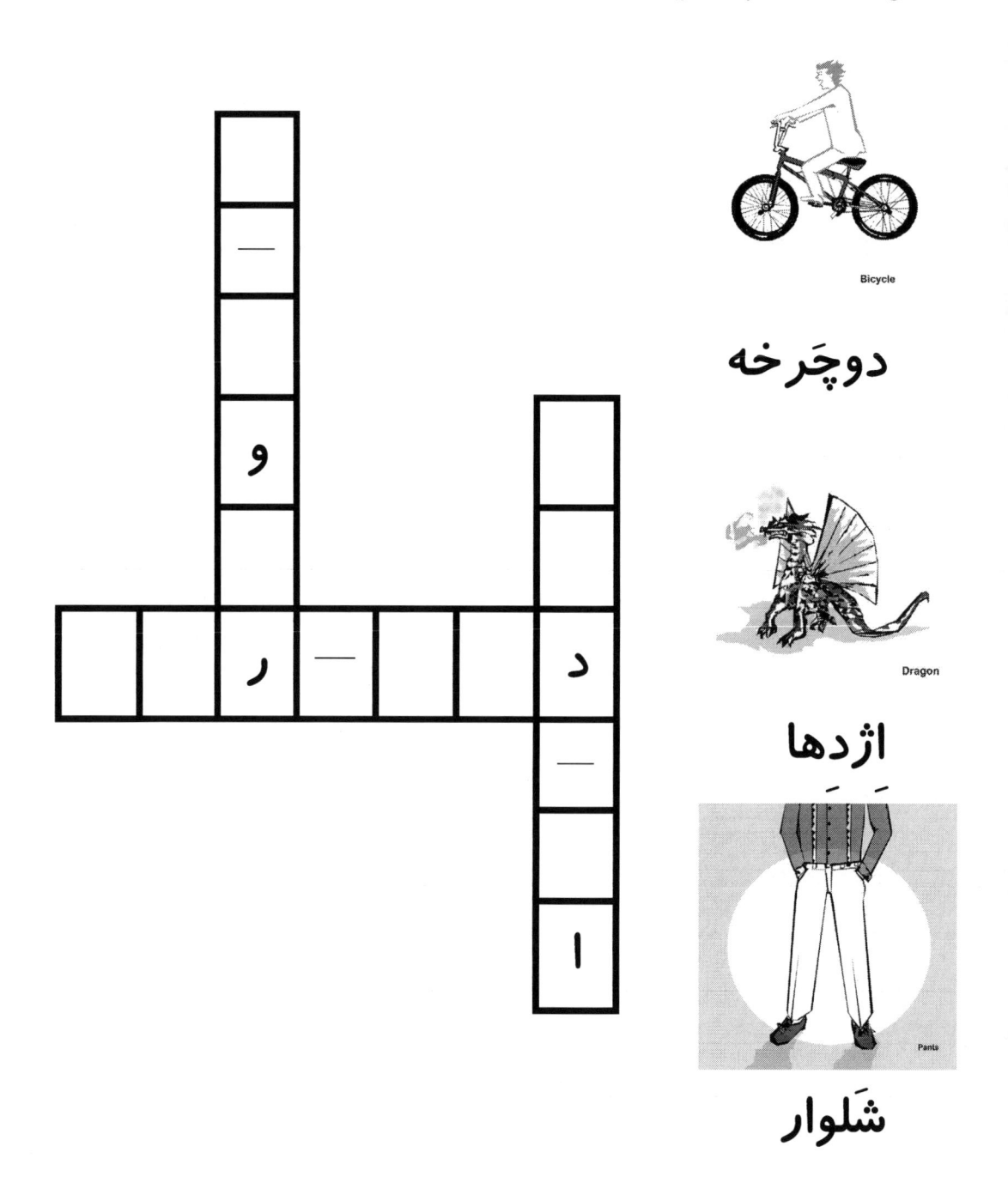

Bicycle

دوچَرخه

Dragon

اژدها

Pants

شَلوار

Find the word below in the puzzle.

دوچَرخه

ل	ص	ش	ا	ه	ف
ه	غ	ا	ر	گَ	ا
ه	خ	ر	چَ	و	د
ه	غ	و	ا	د	پِ
ذ	ص	ر	ق	ت	ف

Look at this picture and write its name under it.

Pants

اِژدها= __ + __ + __ + __ + __ + __

شَلوار= __ + __ + __ + __ + __

دوچَرخه= __ + __ + __ + __ + __ + __ + __

Read the word below and draw a picture of it.

کلمه زیر را بخوان و شکلش را بکش.

اِژدَها

Exercise 19   تمرین ۱۹

خوانَنده

(k̆aa. nan. de)

نَقّاش

(nağ. ğaash)

زَرّافه

(zar. raa. fe)

Read the word for each picture and write the letters in their places.

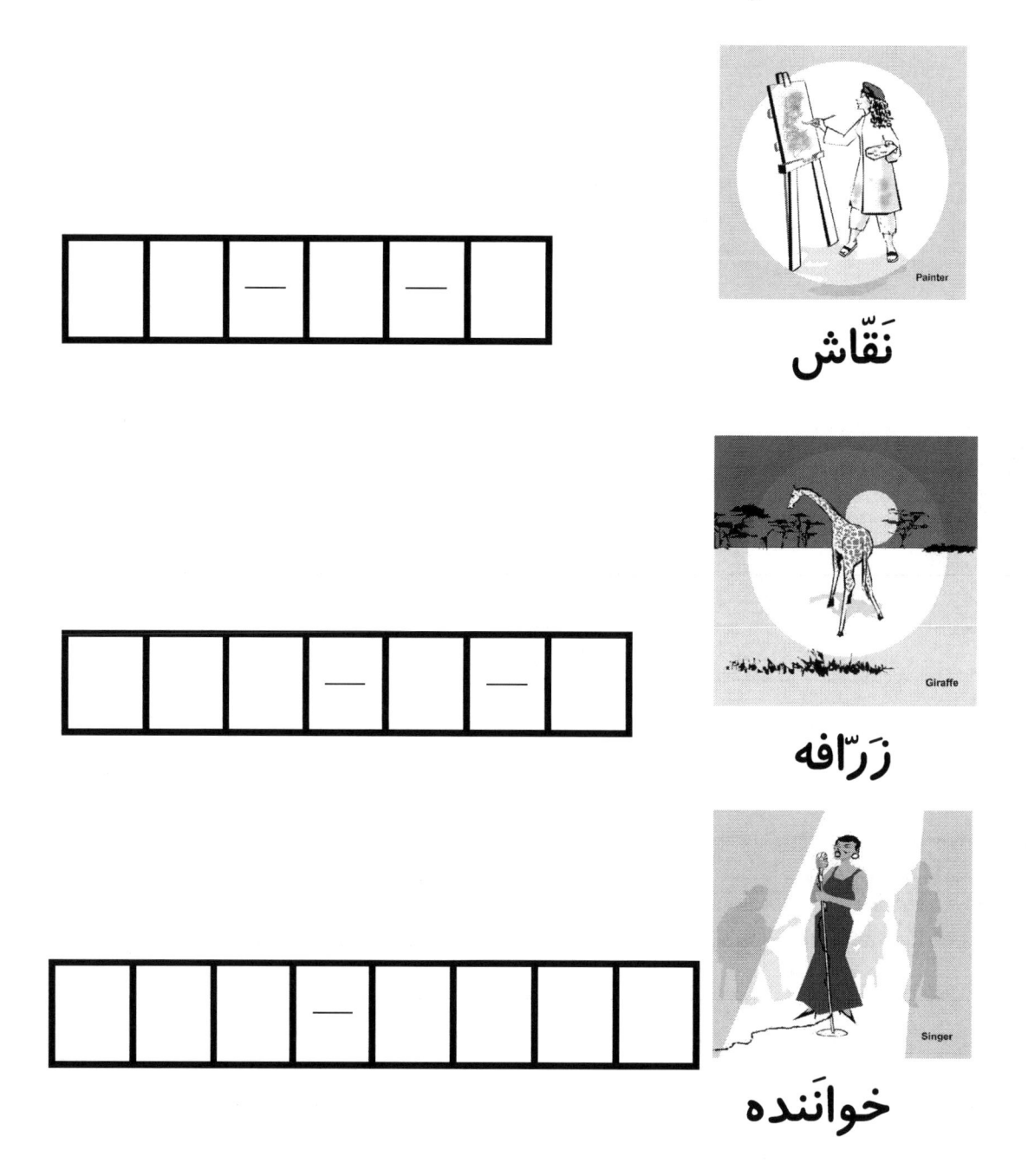

با کمک شکل ها، هر کلمه را بخوان و صداهایش را در جدولِ روبرویش بنویس.

Painter

نَقّاش

Giraffe

زَرّافه

Singer

خوانَنده

۱۴۶

Connect each word to its picture. هر کلمه را به شکلش وصل کن.

Painter

دوچَرخه

Dragon

زَرّافه

Giraffe

خوانَنده

Bicycle

اِژدِها

Singer

نَقّاش

Read the word for each picture and
write the letters in the puzzle.

با کمک شکل ها، هر کلمه را بخوان و
جایش را در جدول پیدا کن.

خواننده

زَرّافه

نَقّاش

Find the word below in the puzzle.   کلمه زیر را در جدول پیدا کن.

نَقّاش

س	اَ	زَ	و	ل	ه	ف
م	ر	ش	ا	قّ	زَ	خ
ا	گ	و	ش	قّ	ل	ه
ر	و	ن	گ	ی	اِ	ل
اَ	ر	ذ	ب	ص	و	پ

Look at this picture and write its name under it.

به این شکل نگاه کن و اسمش را زیر آن بنویس.

Singer

———————————————

Write the letters for each word.

نَقّاش=___ + ___ + ___ + ___ + ___ + ___

زَرّافه=___ + ___ + ___ + ___ + ___ + ___ + ___

خوانَنده=___ + ___ + ___ + ___ + ___ + ___ + ___ + ___

Read the word below and draw a picture of it.

کلمه زیر را بخوان و شکلش را بکش.

زَرّافه

Exercise 20

تمرین ۲۰

صَندَلی

(san. da. lee)

عَصا

('a. saa)

عینَک

('ey. naْk)

Read the word for each picture and write the letters in their places.

با کمک شکل ها، هر کلمه را بخوان و صداهایش را در جدولِ روبرویش بنویس.

عَصا

عینَک

صَندَلی

Connect each word to its picture.

زَرّافه

عَصا

نَقّاش

عِینَک

صَندَلی

Read the word for each picture and write the letters in the puzzle.

با کمک شکل ها، هر کلمه را بخوان و جایش را در جدول پیدا کن.

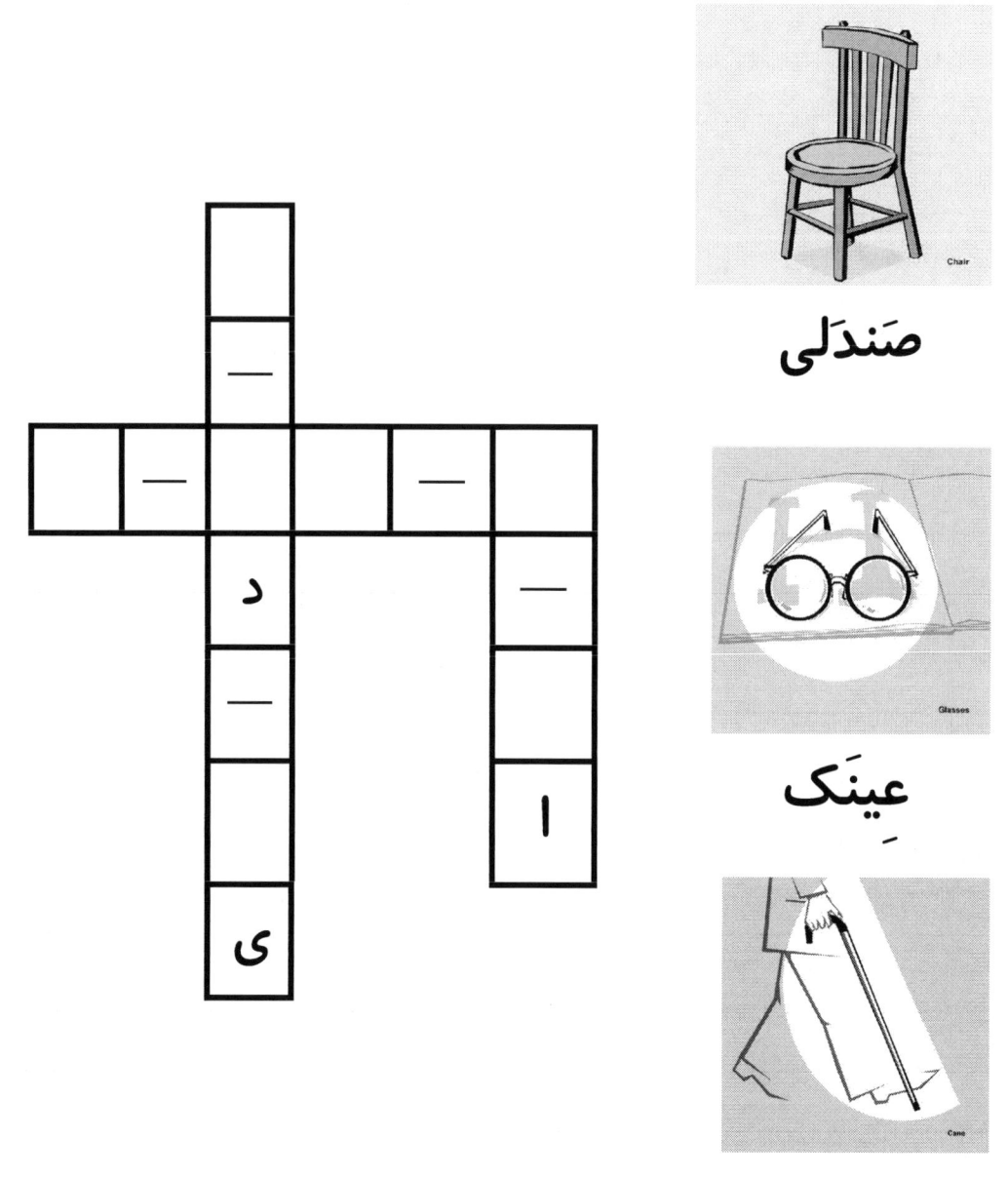

صَندَلی

عِینَک

عَصا

Find the word below in the puzzle.

عینَک

ب	ز	ط	ف	يِ	بِ	چ
د	ا	کَ	ز	و	ا	کُ
ظ	ک	زَ	یِ	ءِ	پ	ذ
ض	يِ	ی	مُ	ه	خ	ا
ی	ز	ا	ت	ح	بِ	ه

Look at this picture and write its name
under it.

به این شکل نگاه کن و اسمش را زیر آن بنویس.

Cane

——————————————

Write the letters for each word.

عَصا= __ + __ + __ + __

عِینَک= __ + __ + __ + __ + __ + __

صَندَلی= __ + __ + __ + __ + __ + __ + __

Read the word below and draw a picture of it.

صَندَلی

Exercise 21   تمرين ٢١

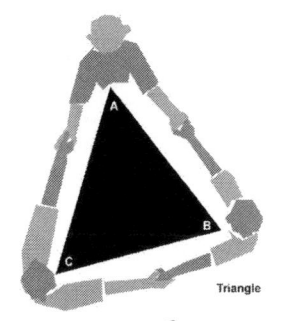

Triangle

مُثَلَّث

(mo. sal. las)

Snail

حَلَزون

(ha. la. zoon)

Couch

مُبل

(mobl)

Read the word for each picture and
write the letters in their places.

با کمک شکل ها، هر کلمه را بخوان و
صداهایش را در جدولِ روبرویش بنویس.

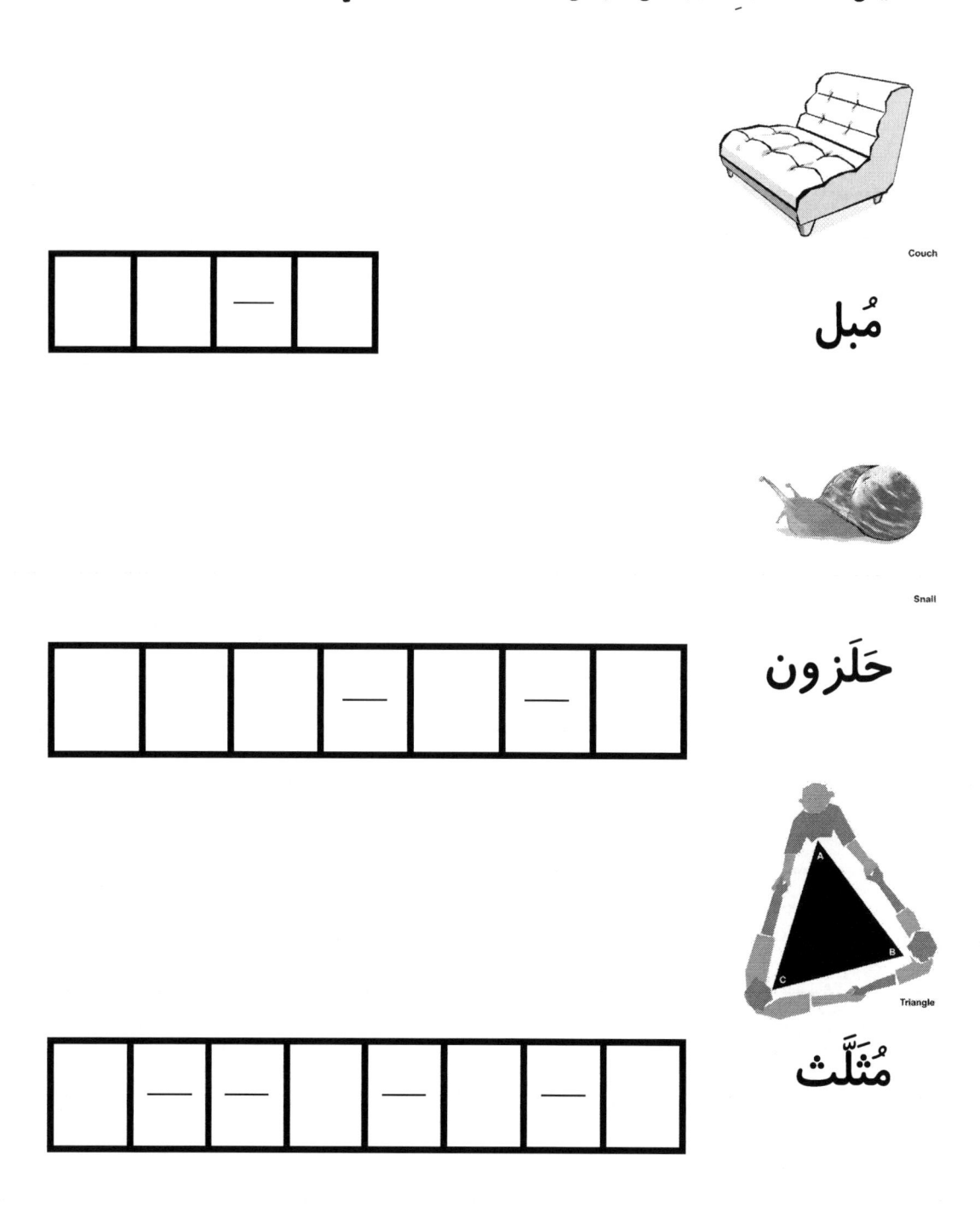

مُبل

Couch

حَلَزون

Snail

مُثَلَّث

Triangle

Connect each word to its picture.　　　　هر کلمه را به شکلش وصل کن.

صَندَلی

مُبل

عِینَک

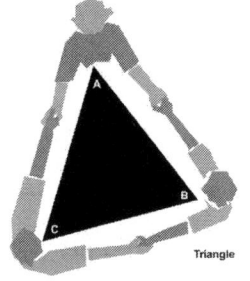

حَلَزون

مُثَلَّث

Read the word for each picture and
write the letters in the puzzle.

با کمک شکل ها، هر کلمه را بخوان و جایش را در جدول پیدا کن.

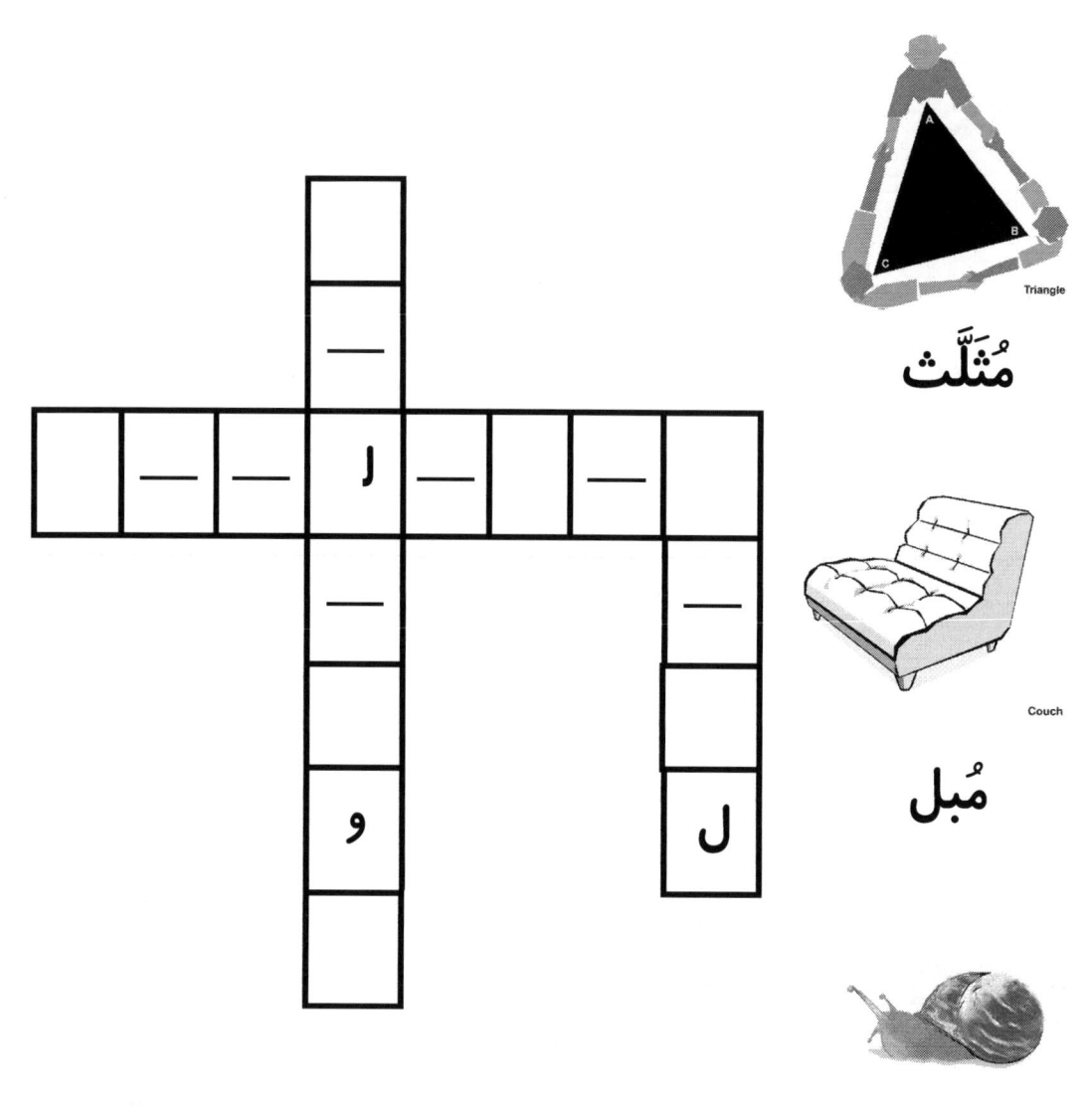

Triangle

مُثَلَّث

Couch

مُبل

Snail

حَلَزون

Find the word below in the puzzle.

کلمه زیر را در جدول پیدا کن.

مُثَلَّث

ک	ث	اَّ	ثَُ	مُ	ا
ا	ظ	س	مُ	ا	بُ
ه	ا	و	ثَُ	س	بَ
ک	ل	ؤُ	ا	و	ز
ل	ج	س	ت	ا	چُ

Look at this picture and write its name under it.

به این شکل نگاه کن و اسمش را زیر آن بنویس.

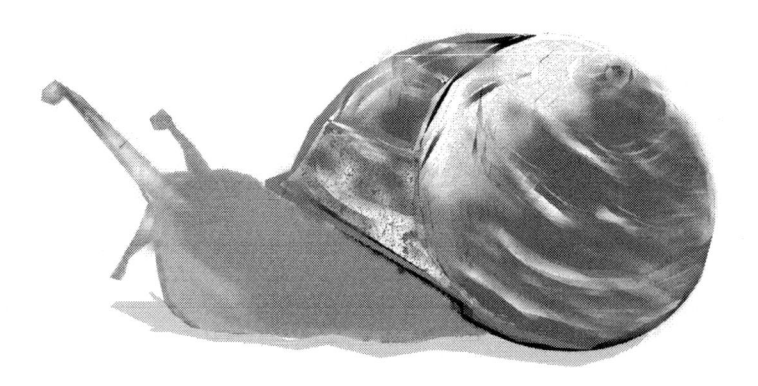

Snail

————————————

مُبل= __ + __ + __ + __

حَلَزون= __ + __ + __ + __ + __ + __ + __

مُثَلَّث= __ + __ + __ + __ + __ + __ + __ + __

Read the word below and draw a picture of it.

مُبل

Exercise 22

قاضی

(ğaa. zee)

چاقو

(chaa. ğoo)

حوض

(hoz)

Read the word for each picture and
write the letters in their places.

با کمک شکل ها، هر کلمه را بخوان و
صداهایش را در جدولِ روبرویش بنویس.

حوض

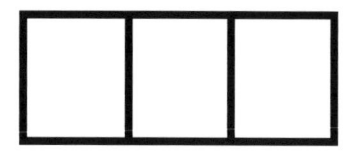

چاقو

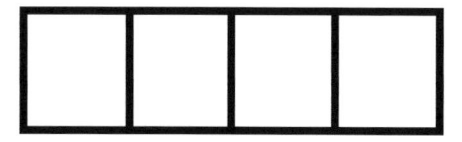

قاضی

Connect each word to its picture. | هر کلمه را به شکلش وصل کن.

Knife

قاضی

Snail

مُثَلَّث

Judge

چاقو

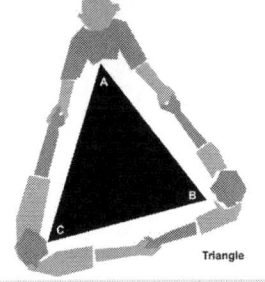
Triangle

حوض

Pond

حَلَزون

Read the word for each picture and
write the letters in the puzzle.

با کمک شکل ها، هر کلمه را بخوان و
جایش را در جدول پیدا کن.

حوض

قاضی

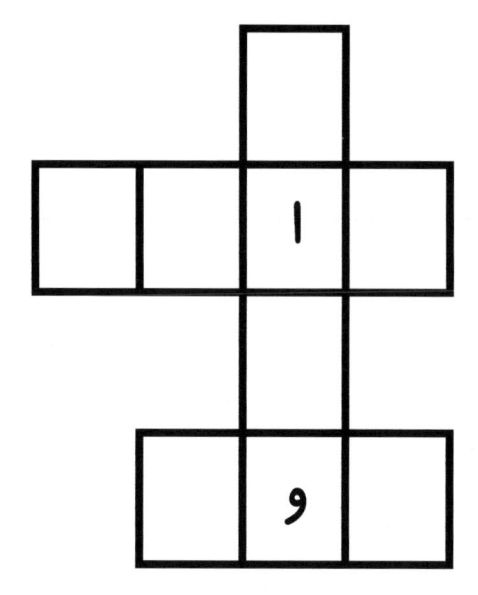

چاقو

Find the word below in the puzzle.

حوض

ز	ف	ا	ل	ر	ه	ا
ب	ح	ث	ه	پ	ا	ج
ت	و	ا	ژ	م	چَ	د
ه	ض	ر	ا	و	د	ن
ر	چُ	ا	و	د	ل	ر

Look at this picture and write its name
under it.

به این شکل نگاه کن و اسمش را زیر آن

بنویس.

Judge

حوض = __ + __ + __

چاقو = __ + __ + __ + __

قاضی = __ + __ + __ + __

چاقو

Exercise 23

طَبل

(tabl)

طَناب

(ta. naab)

طوطی

(too. tee)

Read the word for each picture and write the letters in their places.

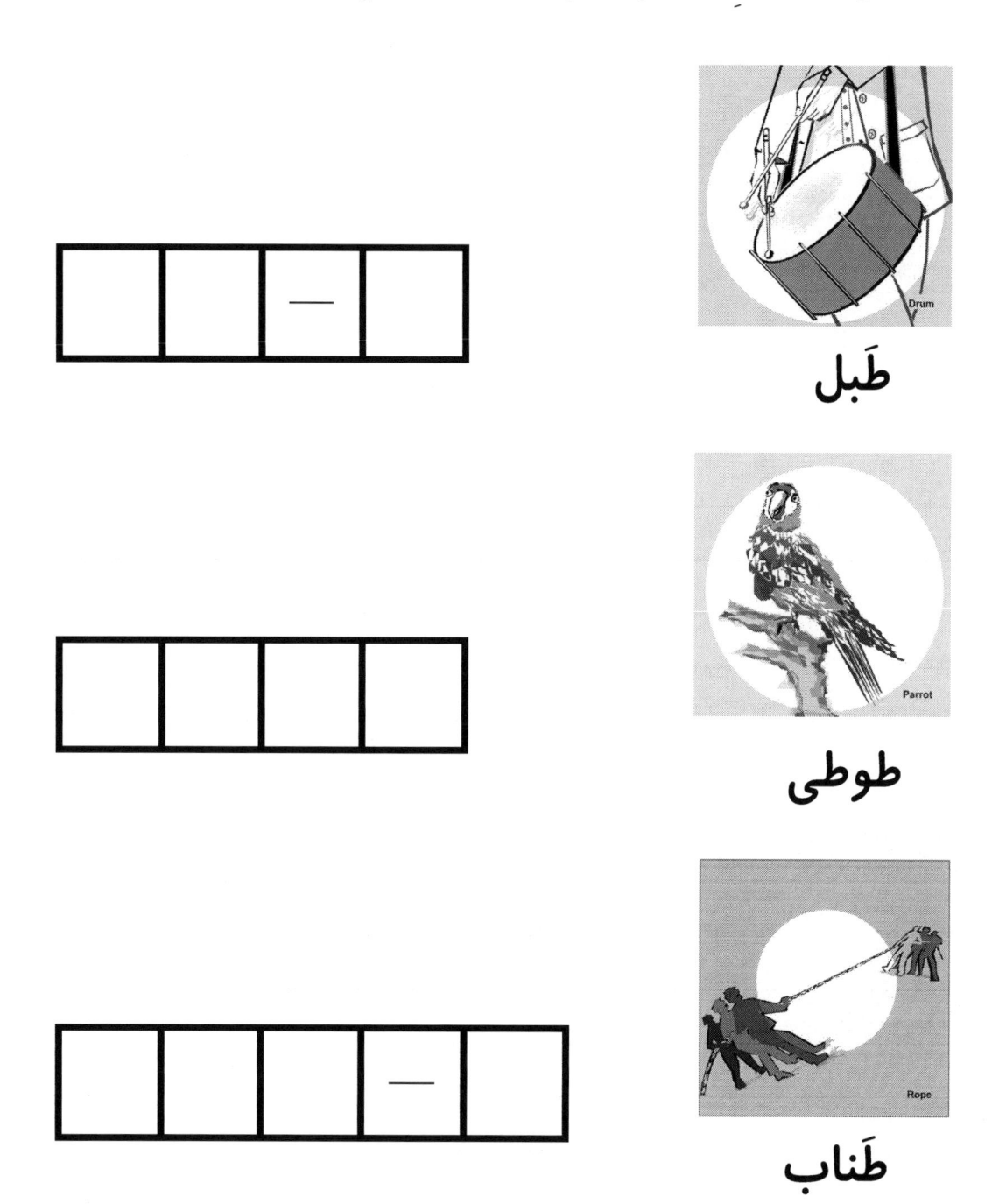

با کمک شکل ها، هر کلمه را بخوان و صداهایش را در جدولِ روبرویش بنویس.

طَبل

طوطی

طَناب

هر کلمه را به شکلش وصل کن.

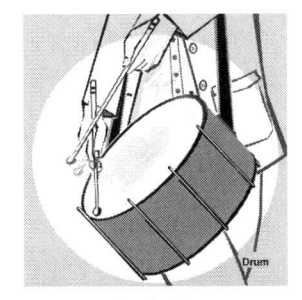

قاضی

حوض

طَبل

طوطی

طَناب

Read the word for each picture and write the letters in the puzzle.

با کمک شکل ها، هر کلمه را بخوان و جایش را در جدول پیدا کن.

طوطی

طَناب

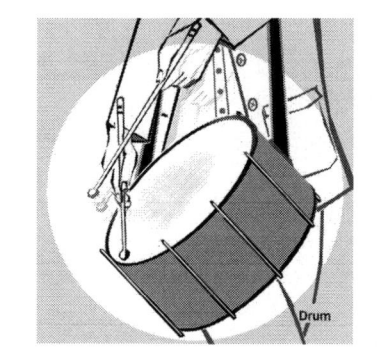

طَبل

		ا		—	
					و
			—		

طَناب

ب	ه	و	ر	ه	ا	تۡ
ا	ر	ف	طَ	ا	تۡ	بۡ
ک	سـ	بۡ	ا	زۡ	و	م
و	ب	ا	زۡ	طَ	ر	ک
ن	م	ر	زۡ	گ	تۡ	ا

Look at this picture and write its name under it.

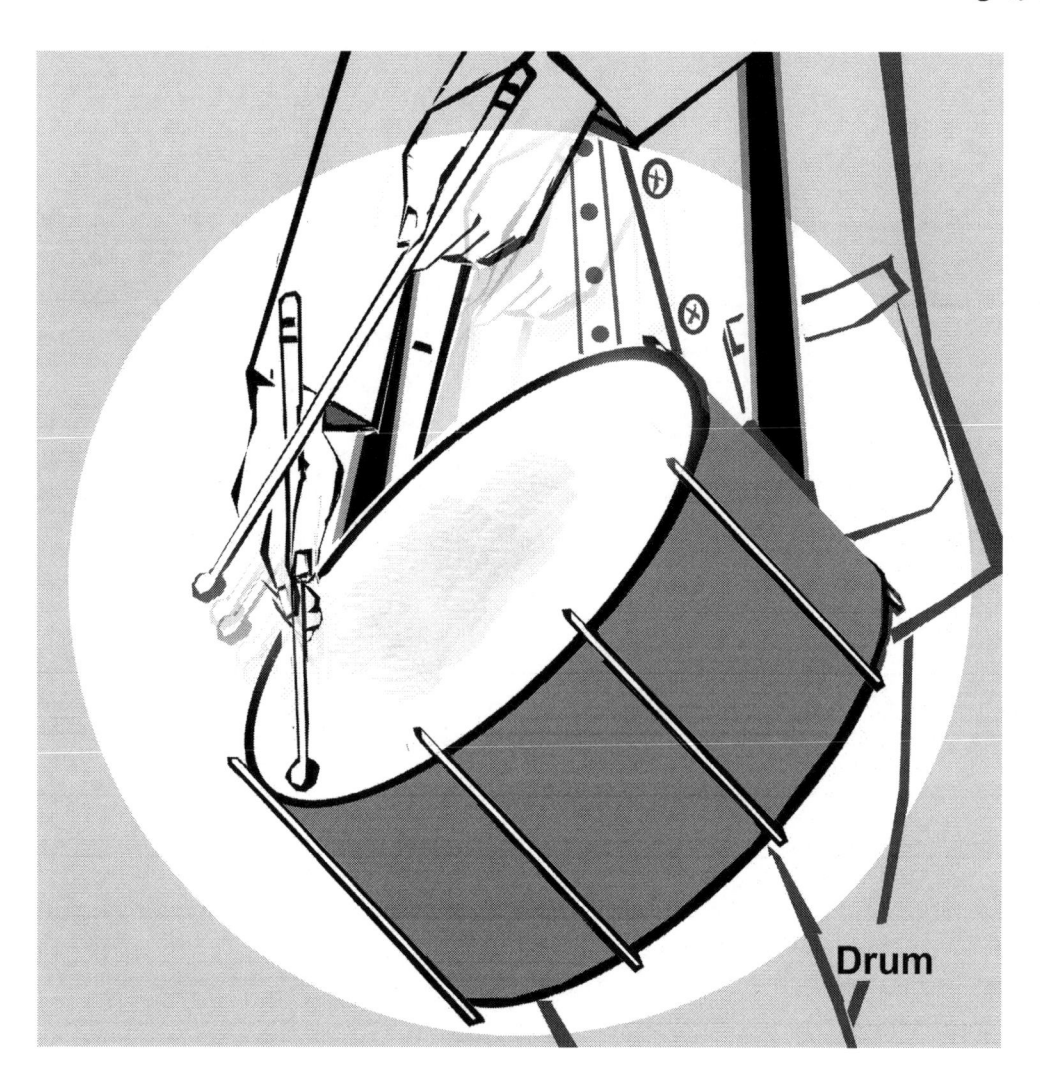

Drum

_____

Write the letters for each word. صداهای هر کلمه را بنویس.

طَبل= __ + __ + __ + __

طوطی= __ + __ + __ + __

طَناب= __ + __ + __ + __ + __

Read the word below and draw a picture of it.

کلمه زیر را بخوان و شکلش را بکش.

طوطی

Exercise 24 — تمرین ۲۴

کَلاغ

(ka. laağ)

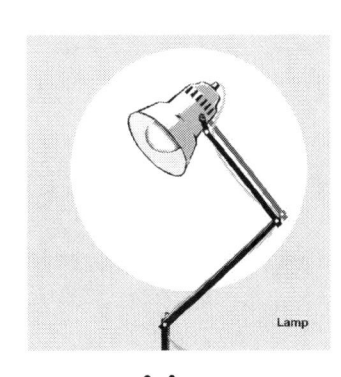

چراغ

(che. r̄aağ)

ظُروف

(zo. roof)

Read the word for each picture and write the letters in their places.

با کمک شکل‌ها، هر کلمه را بخوان و صداهایش را در جدولِ روبرویش بنویس.

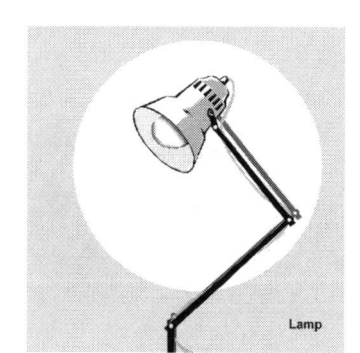

Lamp

چِراغ

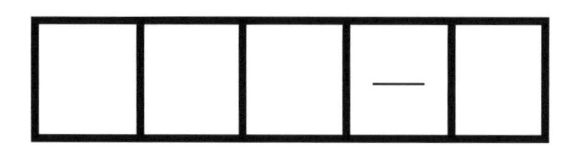

Dishes

ظُروف

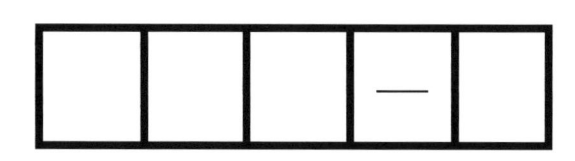

Crow

کَلاغ

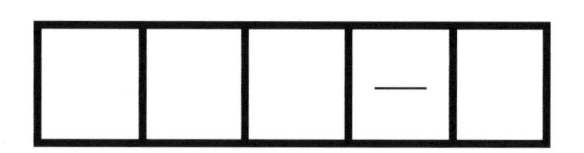

چِراغ

طَبل

طوطی

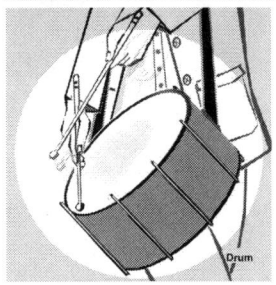

ظُروف

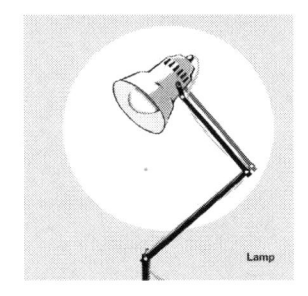

کَلاغ

Read the word for each picture and write the letters in the puzzle.

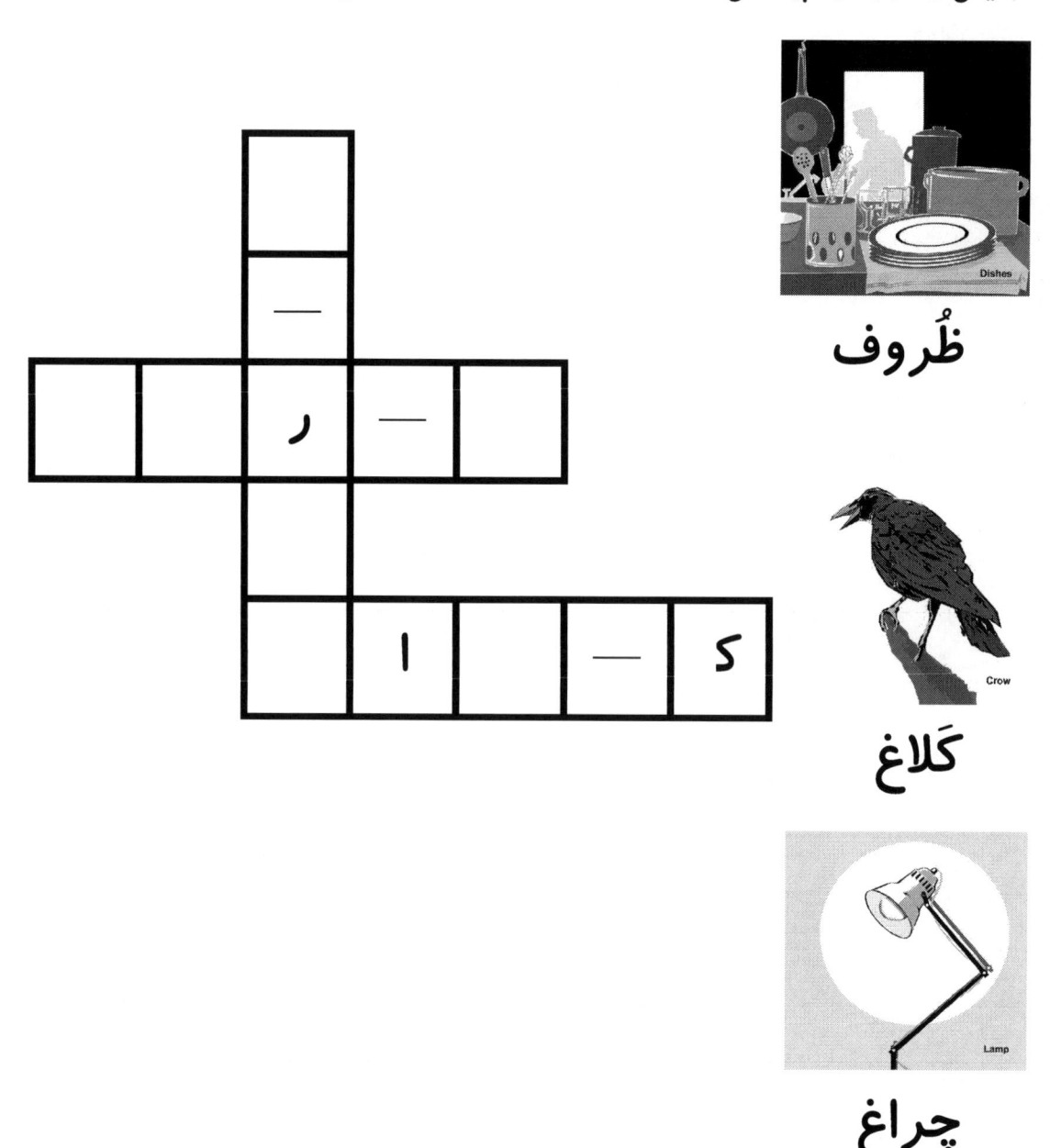

ظُروف

کَلاغ

چِراغ

Find the word below in the puzzle.

کلمه زیر را در جدول پیدا کن.

ظُروف

ش	مُ	ا	بِ	مَ	س
ه	ف	و	ر	ظُ	ا
ل	ر	ظُ	و	ه	ف
ا	ل	ش	ه	ق	ی
چ	ر	طُ	ذ	ا	ف

Look at this picture and write its name under it.

به این شکل نگاه کن و اسمش را زیر آن بنویس.

Crow

———————————————

Write the letters for each word. صداهای هر کلمه را بنویس.

چِراغ= __ + __ + __ + __ + __

کَلاغ= __ + __ + __ + __ + __

ظُروف= __ + __ + __ + __ + __

Read the word below and draw a picture of it.

کلمه زیر را بخوان و شکلش را بکش.

چِراغ

Exercise 25 تمرین ۲۵

Hen

مُرغ
(morğ)

Paper

کاغَذ
(kaa. ğaz)

Frog

قورباغه
(ğoor. baa. ğe)

Read the word for each picture and
write the letters in their places.

با کمک شکل ها، هر کلمه را بخوان و
صداهایش را در جدول ِ روبرویش بنویس.

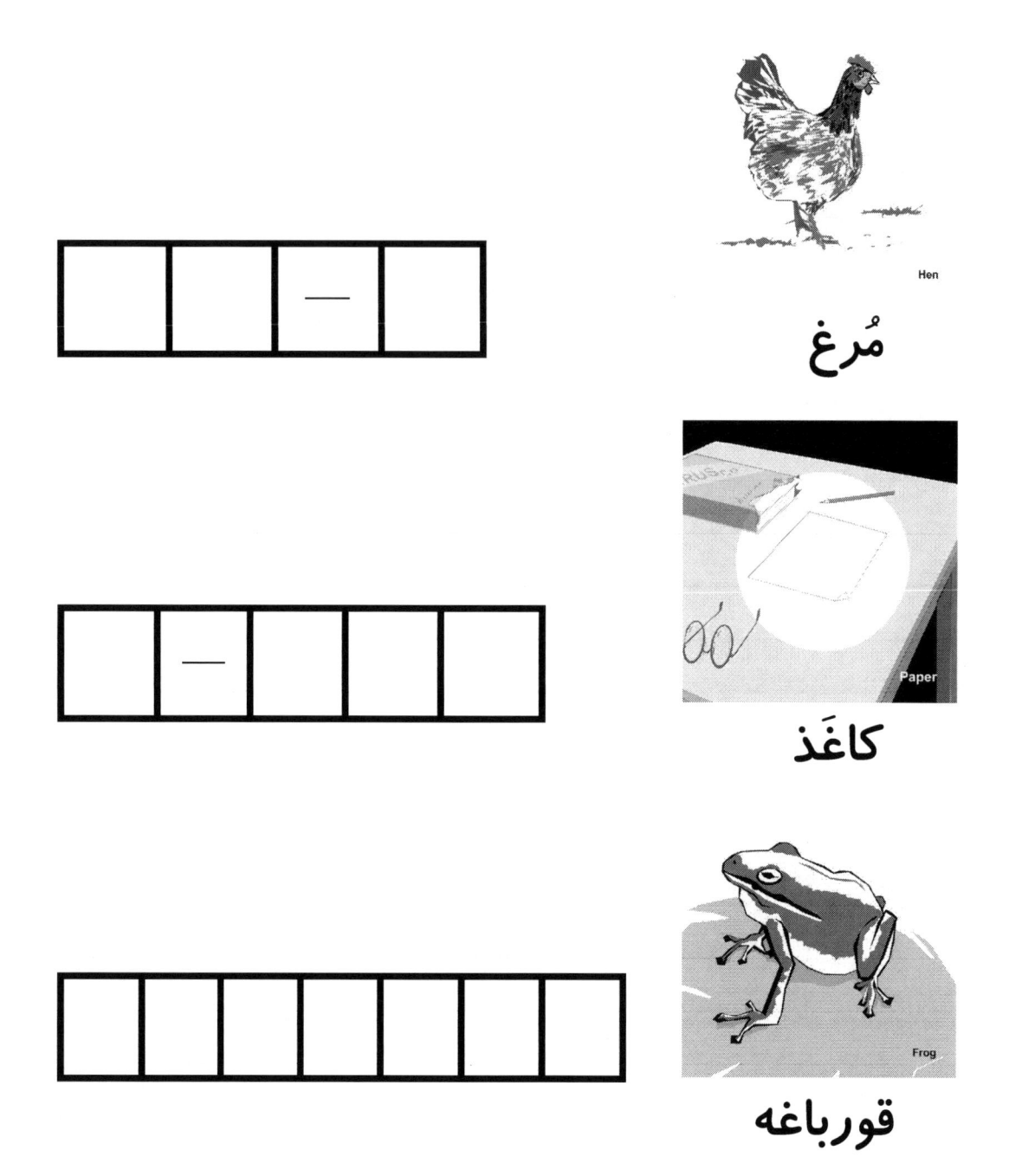

Hen

مُرغ

Paper

کاغَذ

Frog

قورباغه

Connect each word to its picture. هر کلمه را به شکلش وصل کن.

کَلاغ

قورباغه

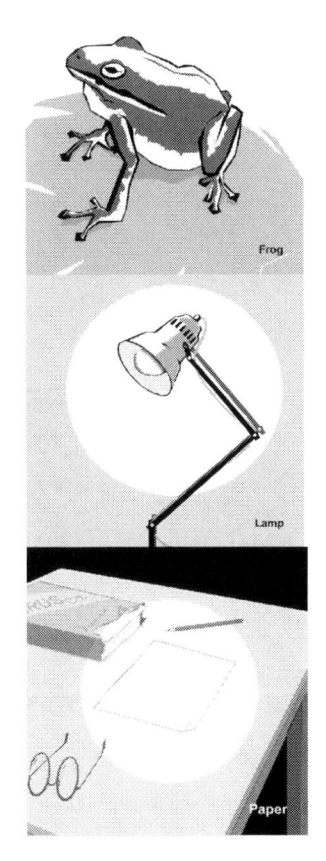

کاغَذ

مُرغ

چِراغ

Read the word for each picture and write the letters in the puzzle.

با کمک شکل ها، هر کلمه را بخوان و جایش را در جدول پیدا کن.

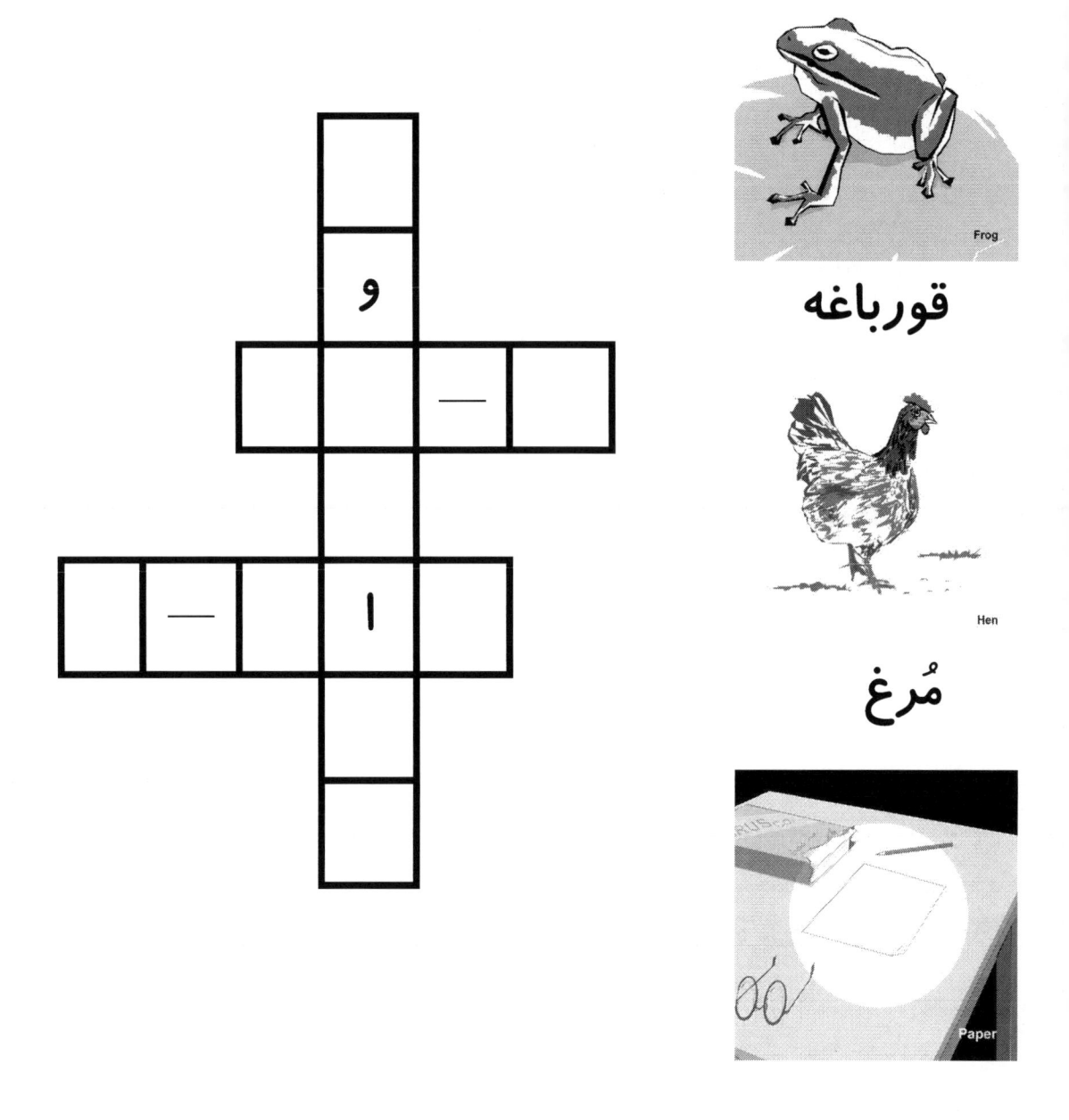

قورباغه

Frog

مُرغ

Hen

Paper

Find the word below in the puzzle.

كلمه زير را در جدول پيدا كن.

كاغَذ

ص	و	ا	ر	ش	و	ى
ل	ه	ذ	غَ	ا	ک	پ
غَ	ى	پ	ا	ت	ک	و
و	ز	عَ	س	ا	ج	ک
ى	ذ	ه	ل	ک	ا	ذ

Look at this picture and write its name under it.

Hen

_____

Write the letters for each word. صداهای هر کلمه را بنویس.

مُرغ = __ + __ + __ + __

کاغَذ = __ + __ + __ + __ + __

قورباغه = __ + __ + __ + __ + __ + __ + __

Read the word below and draw a picture of it.

کلمه زیر را بخوان و شکلش را بکش.

قورباغه

براى آشنایى با سایر کتاب هاى "نشر بهار" از وب سایت این انتشارات دیدن فرمائید.

**To learn more about the other publications of Bahar Books
please visit the website.**

Bahar Books

www.baharbooks.com

Made in the USA
San Bernardino, CA
08 March 2020